A Rose by Another Name

LOCUST HILL LITERARY STUDIES
No. 5

Robert Frost, The Rose Family Man
Courtesy of Lesley Lee Francis—
original in the University of Virginia Library.

A Rose by Another Name

*A Survey of Literary Flora
from Shakespeare to Eco*

Robert F. Fleissner

LOCUST HILL PRESS
West Cornwall, CT
1989

© 1989 Robert F. Fleissner
All rights reserved

Library of Congress Cataloging-in-Publication Data

Fleissner, Robert F.
    A rose by another name : a survey of literary flora from
Shakespeare to Eco / Robert F. Fleissner.
       164p.   cm. — (Locust Hill literary studies ; no. 5)
    Includes bibliographical references.
    ISBN 0-933951-33-7 (lib. bdg. : alk. paper) : $24.00
    1. Roses in literature. 2. Flowers in literature. 3. Herbs in
literature. 4. Literature, Modern—History and criticism.
I. Title. II. Series.
PN56.R75F57 1989
809'.9336—dc20

    Excerpt from "The Hollow Men" in *Collected Poems 1909–1962* by
T. S. Eliot, copyright 1936 by Harcourt Brace Jovanovich, Inc.,
copyright © 1964, 1963 by T. S. Eliot, reprinted by permission of the
publisher.

Printed on acid-free, 250-year-life paper
Manufactured in the United States of America

In loving memory of
my former colleague
OM DIXIT
and his family
killed by a terrorist bombing
over Scotland
1988

"Dr. Om Dixit was a flower of India. He was so willing to help every person on the face of the earth. He was my best friend and colleague for the past twenty years. He helped me in growing. A collection of essays on flowers and literature is a befitting memorial for him indeed."

                              C.S. Rangi
                              Assistant Professor of Mathematics
                              Central State University
                              Wilberforce, Ohio

The Paper Flowers

San Francisco

The sun was in my eyes there on the hill
As with a cry of joy we stood stockstill
    Beside the florist's overwhelming show,
    The flaunting gypsy braggadocio
Of tulip, marigold, and daffodil.

Only a breath of sorcery until
My clearing vision could direct the shrill
    Vulgarity of paper blooms and know
    The sun was in my eyes.

Too crisp the rose, too prim the daisy's frill;
Nowhere a dewdrop sliding down to spill
    Sweetness and send it floating to and fro;
    Then from that lovely cheat to you aglow
Near me I turned, half wondering if still
    The sun was in my eyes.

                    Celeste Turner Wright
                    Seasoned Timber (1977)
                    (reprinted with the
                    permission of the author)

Table of Contents

Introductory Poem: "The Paper Flowers" *vii*
Preface: The Rose Scene *xi*
Foreword by Pierre L. Horn *xix*
Part I: Shakespeare, Roses, and the Like *1*
    Chapter I: As You Like *Rosa*lind; or, "Arden and ... Merry" / Mary Arden: Calling on Shakespeare's Mother in *As You Like It* *7*
    Chapter II: Rosemary in *Romeo and Juliet* and Other Herbs *17*
Part II: Romanticism and Roses *35*
    Chapter III: A Rose by Another Name: The Floral Digression in *The Naval Treaty*—Regrafted *45*
    Chapter IV: The Germination of "Rosebud" in *Citizen Kane:* The Dickensian Bulb *53*
    Chapter V: Opium as the Rose of Love: "Kubla Khan" Revisited *59*
    Chapter VI: "Pot Luck": Drugs and Romanticism *63*
    Chapter VII: Byron's Bypath Back to Xanadu *69*
Part III: Roses and "Modernism": (Stein, Frost, Eliot)—and Maugham *75*
    Chapter VIII: Four Roses and a Stein *79*
    Chapter IX: From Stein to Frost: The Germinal Soil of a Rose Family *85*
    Chapter X: *Sub Rosa*: Focussing on Frost's Flower as "Five-Petaled" *91*
    Chapter XI: Plucking at T. S. Eliot's "Multifoliate Rose" and Hollowness *99*
    Chapter XII: A Rose Window on *Human Bondage*: An Overview of Its Onomastics *103*

Part IV: Roses and Special Effects *117*

    Chapter XIII: Henry Constable's "My Lady's Presence Makes the Roses Red": A Reappraisal *121*

    Chapter XIV: *Die Rose ist ohne Warum?* The Name of *The Name of the Rose* *131*

    Chapter XV: Roses and the Arts: A Humanistic and Horticultural *Engagement* *137*

Afterword by the Rev. Théodore Koehler, S.M. *147*

Concluding Poem: "The Black Rose" *149*

Index *151*

Preface

The Rose Scene

In an oddly out-of-character episode, perhaps an uncharacteristic moment of laxity, it would appear, the master sleuth Sherlock Holmes once turned from intense consideration of the theft of a British naval treaty to a brief disquisition on the *je ne sais quoi* of the rose. He aptly remarked that this flower of flowers has no purpose other than being decorative. The theme of his brief meditation was that what moderns might now caption Rose Power is primal evidence revealing the loving presence of the Creator. Hence the rose amply glorifies the marvelous beneficence of eternal Providence. Analogously, we recall roses miraculously blooming out of season in Franz Werfel's popular novel translated as *The Song of Bernadette* (also memorably filmed). Yet specialized scholarship has hardly been satisfied with such a simple exegesis of Holmes's credo. Critics have demurred that he thereby degenerated into a sentimentalist, that in particular he failed to discern the evident botanical justification of the flower: not to decorate, but to propagate its species, that being the principal *raison d'être* for its aroma. Or, as one Holmes specialist has a bit tersely put it, it is obligated to attract insect fertilizers.[1] How mundane such critics can be.

In answer to such secular minds, let us suggest that rather more background is needed for studying such rose symbolism. Even Sir Arthur Conan Doyle was partially dependent on a previous sleuth—not Poe's Chevalier Dupin this time, but Collins's Sergeant Cuff. This connection is not cited in a recent survey of mystery story writings of Victorian times in the chapters dealing with Collins and Conan Doyle,[2] though the author does cite a passage from *The Moonstone* which inevitably anticipates Holmes: "when it comes to unravelling a mystery there isn't the equal in England of Sergeant Cuff!"[3]

In any event, the leading work on Collins and Conan Doyle is a scarce monograph published in Sweden and not very accessible.[4] Hence regrettably it cannot be cited here. But Chapter III of this book will try to make up for that.

Using this Holmesian *début* as a starter, let us next invite rose imagery in larger, metaphoric contexts. Because Dante's, and subsequently his disciple T.S. Eliot's, uses of such symbolism are already common knowledge (notably in the *Paradiso* of *The Divine Comedy* as then reverberated in *Four Quartets*), let us call to mind other literary rosarians. Similarly, because Edmund Waller ("Go, Lovely Rose"), Robert Burns ("O my Luv's like a red, red rose"), William Blake ("The Sick Rose"), and then the Romantics in general are rather well known for praising this flower, our focus may well reside on more unusual floral connoisseurs.

So let us start with Shakespeare, touching on woman as rose in Rosalind of *As You Like It*, then latterly (as the title demands) on *Romeo and Juliet*, but on flowers *per se* only inasmuch as the heroine's oft-quoted "rose by any other name" uncovers Nature's amplitude in the play in the form of a literary herbarium, a metaphoric gathering of simples.[5] Yet, on the more subliminal level, we first must spade up the fertile rose element in *As You Like It*, trusting not to be pricked by some of its thorny subtleties, particularly regarding the name of Rosalind (never to be confounded onomastically with Rosaline, Romeo's discard). Indeed, Shakespeare had much to say about our general floral subject (to which the Shakespearean gardens in, say, Stratford-upon-Avon attest) and on the rose in particular, notably his War of the Roses with weak Richard II its original instigator as "that sweet, lovely rose." Still, the most substantial "rose by another name" with the Avon master is more herbal than religious.

After historically cultivating Shakespeare and the flowering Renaissance, we meditate on "Romanticism and Roses" and allied concerns. After correlating Holmes and Cuff in a preliminary chapter to set the scene, we proceed to the relation of other literary flora (hence the deliberate blanket designation of this book's subtitle), specifically apropos of hard drugs, as in the section with the ironic, admittedly somewhat satiric label of "Pot Luck." (Its initial stimulus had a pedagogical vintage.) Then because of Charles Dickens's own rose-like creations, such as Rose Maylie, Rosa Dartle, but conspicuously Rosa Bud of *The Mystery of Edwin Drood*, we can see in this one-time most popular novelist a probable source even for the

Preface xiii

tantalizing Rosebud riddle in *Citizen Kane*. Although, strictly, Dickens was not Romantic but Victorian—likewise Collins and Conan Doyle—they fit under the rubric of Romanticism in its larger sense because their quest for mysteries tells of a kind of late, as well as latent British Romanticism, a sort rampant enough throughout the end of the last century.

In Section III, we close ranks with our own times, Orson Welles's cinematic masterpiece serving as a suitable transition from II. Since the essay on that film was first drafted, the verdict that the first two versions of the script were by his associate Herman Mankiewicz has come more to light; in a letter to *The Listener* (29 May 1980), the latter's son claimed that not Welles but his partner had "entirely written" the script. Then, in a new biography, Barbara Leaming has remarked instead that "Welles' old teacher, Roger Hill, turned up a play called Marching Song that was written by Orson at 17" and that in it "is the basic structure of *Kane*."[6] Who then is closer to the truth?

In keeping with the time-honored collector's habit of glamorizing literary subjects by binding them together in the form of bouquet (a courtly tradition harking back to the Renaissance), the title and subtitle of this collection are meant to supply a horticultural metaphor for binding together the diverse essays that follow. The purpose has been to follow the proposal offered me once by the editor of the poetry magazine *Flame*: "Give the reader a spade and let him plant a garden with it." In a word, why not consider a liter*al* spade as a liter*ary* one and dig for richer floral roots? This book tries to do just that—with hopes that the reader as literary gardener will have a requisite green thumb.

The purpose of the arrangement set up is chronological but not meant merely that way, rather to show how the symbol of the rose has evolved: from the flora in *Romeo and Juliet* and spiritual resonances in *As You Like It*, to Romantic variations on the rosarian theme (including the Neo-Romanticism of Orson Welles and Mankiewicz), and finally to "modernist" preoccupations, some of which are harking back, on one level, to medieval origins whereas others deal with very modern, relevant significance. The final section involves closer reading of rose imagery from both Renaissance and modern perspectives. A kind of final coda appears in a report of an unusual rose conference in the southeastern Ohio area, not one of the ordinary horticultural variety alone but involving national prizewinners, keynoted by an internationally known authority or two, and focussing finally on a one-time worldwide bestseller, *Il Nome della Rosa* (*The Name of the Rose*). The overall progression is therefore from the concrete to the abstract, as it might well be for the thoughtful, even as, philosophically, the study of epistemology itself corroborates man's vital need for abstracting from sense data to arrive at universal conclusions.

Although a few of the chapters have already appeared in unrevised, early draft form in specialized journals, not only nationally (as a version of the Stein essay in *Journal of Modern Literature*) but elsewhere (as in the annual *Marianum*, published by the Pontifical Faculty of the Vatican in Rome), these have all undergone major surgery before having been admitted here. The purpose in revising was partly to show that individually oriented essays written for special occasion and audiences might finally interrelate in terms of a general rosarian theme. In any case, although many of these journals are authoritative in their field, unhappily they are not so accessible to the ordinary library visitor.

The main purpose of the collection is to give the innovative reader and rose-lover a comprehensive survey of floral symbolism in *belles lettres* by stressing major authors and works in an intensely documented and variegated manner. This arrangement may not be on quite the same level as Betty Pavey's authoritative study on rose arrangement entitled *Say It with Roses*, but material appealing to both generalist and specialist is included, and sentimentality is shunned. Hence mysticism is played off against plain mystery, documented research on herbal lore against light-hearted approaches to opium as the rose of love. Even though the approach may be more decorative, say, than in-depth at times, the moral meaning is always central, as it should be. Shakespeare's early comedy and tragedy can be reread or seen reënacted as not so much immature as florally based upon his Warwickshire countryside, where he grew up, both physically and spiritually. For the question of his possible early Catholicism enters the picture—a major issue posed recently again by E.A.J. Honigmann in his new, important study of *Shakespeare: The "Lost Years."*[7]

By visualizing the extent to which his plays relate not only to natural but supernatural law, we can get a better comprehension of their significance. They then might be used as stepping stones for better coping with his later plays having more sophisticated religious backdrops like *Measure for Measure*. In the same way, the essays dealing with floral subject-matter in the last century have their thematic purpose, helping us to grasp the intrinsic meaning of literary creations. Because the attractive poppy relates aesthetically to the rose, we consider Coleridge and the opiate effects in his memorable "Kubla Khan." This "rose of love" also indirectly relates to mystery literature (as in Collins and Conan Doyle, whose model detective was himself on drugs for a spate), to Dickens's last, uncompleted mystery novel (with its well-known opiate theme), to Orson Welles (who obviously transformed "Kubla Khan" but also the Dickens work in his *Citizen Kane*), and to Byron (who fits into the Xanaduvian tradition himself). Even though, pedagogically, the subject of drugs has to be considered with care in the classroom nowadays, its overall relevance to modern students cannot be denied.

Likewise Stein's roses need to be seen rearranged if only because of the enormous impact she has had upon Modernism. The influence of modern Symbolism, for example, can scarcely be discussed in terms of its French roots without mentioning her pervasive influence. The effect of her work—epitomized by her rose line—ranges far and wide, even encompassing Umberto Eco's stimulating rose novel of recent years. As for Frost, he was clearly indebted to Stein in "The Rose Family," but the full impact of his satirical rendering can be understood only if his debt to Austin Dobson is likewise taken into account, as will be revealed. On the other hand, his inherent symbolism stands on its own as harking back even to medieval times with its recondite, even numerological concerns. Even more so, Eliot's rose symbolism reflects past times, in this case the more doctrinally Christian past. Lastly, an anagogical overtone, one encompassing Judaism as well as Christianity, is discernible in the rose symbolism (here broadly related to onomastics) in Maugham.

Among the papers hitherto unpublished are complementary ones such as the Maugham study just mentioned, the second Shakespearean analysis, and the close study of Constable's "My Lady's Presence Makes the Roses Red." Although, true, numerous book-length studies on flora in Shakespeare in general are sequestered away in the libraries, the herbal approach to *Romeo and Juliet* provides one unifying meaning for the tragedy as a whole—not a very Aristotelian one, but then the historical evidence is that Shakespeare knew little about the Stagyrite. The essay on Maugham opens a rose window on the hitherto untouched garden of his onomatology in his most popular novel, *Of Human Bondage*, showing that he was indeed a subliminal master of names. The more technical study of the text of Constable's sonnet rehabilitates this early sonneteer.

Although much has been written on flora in Shakespeare before, if not with the precise approach taken here, almost nothing has been comprehensively composed on the other floral subjects under consideration, even Rosebud in *Citizen Kane*. Emphasis upon a particular genre or period by itself would have had the stultifying effect of making our subject too specialized and narrow. What counts or justifies this undertaking is the universal. If not everything has this pertinent universal value, the reader at least is free to arrive at that critical decision for himself.

Lastly, it is imperative to mention that these essays have been written over the course of several years and in diverse contexts, hence for many different occasions and audiences, thus accounting for some fairly obvious variations in style and approach. For example, the largely academic aspects of the opening chapters are meant to be taken in counterpoint to the rather more informal focus of some succeeding ones. To some valid extent, such a contrast is simply one basic to the different overall styles of the historical periods being discussed and is therefore to be expected. In any event, it is the author's fervent hope that the stylistic differences may be finally seen as adding helpful variety to a generally hypnotic subject and thus may ultimately be taken as an asset.

Some of the material in the pages that follow has appeared in *Journal of Modern Literature, Names, Marianum, Ohioana Quarterly, Colby Library Quarterly,* and *The Explicator,* and our thanks are expressed to the editors of these journals for permission to reprint in revised form. Many thanks also to Pierre L. Horn and Cecile Cary of Wright State University for proofreading and some minor editing. The Ohio Humanities Council is to be applauded again for its support of the Rose conference at Central State University, Ohio, which led to this floral adventure. The stimulus of the discovery of the remains of the Rose Theatre in London in 1988 was also the *cause célèbre* for this book. Special thanks are due to Dr. Alfred Dorn, twice Vice President of the Poetry Society of America, for permission to use his unpublished poem "The Black Rose." Robert Frost's "The Rose Family" copyright © 1928 by Holt, Rinehart and Winston, Inc. and renewed 1956 by Robert Frost. Reprinted from *The Poetry of Robert*

Preface xvii

Frost, edited Edward Connery Lathem, by permission of Henry Holt and Company, Inc. Excerpts from "The Hollow Men" from *Collected Poems 1909-1962*, by T. S. Eliot, copyright 1936 by Harcourt Brace Jovanovich, Inc.; copyright © 1964, 1965 by T. S. Eliot. Reprinted by permission of the publisher. Thanks also are due to Rob Kohn (herbalist, former colleague, play director, actor), *No Common Scents*, Yellow Springs, Ohio, for valuable advice.

—R.F.F.

Springfield, Ohio
(formerly: "Rose Capital of the World")

Notes

1. See D. Martin Dakin's authoritative *Sherlock Holmes Commentary* (New York: Drake, 1972), p. 136.

2. Audrey Peterson, *Victorian Masters of Mystery: From Wilkie Collins to Conan Doyle* (New York: Frederick Ungar, 1984).

3. Peterson, p. 61.

4. S.B. Liljegren, *The Parentage of Sherlock Holmes* (Stockholm: Almqvist and Wiksell, 1971).

5. For a useful, related article, see Charles R. Forker, "The Green Underworld of Early Shakespearean Tragedy," *Shakespeare Studies*, 17 (1985), 25-47.

6. *Orson Welles* (New York: Viking, 1985)—as cited in a review-article in the Springfield (Ohio) *News-Sun* (14 Oct. 1985).

7. Manchester: Manchester University Press, 1985.

Foreword

From the beginning flowers have offered enchanted observers examples of natural beauty in chiseled miniature form, so much so that the Greeks often imagined their myriad nymphs and heroes metamorphosed into flowers. Among these we can name the tender Acantha and the self-loving Narcissus, an all-too-impatient Crocus and the unfortunate Hyacinthus, or Clytie, who out of faithful love for Apollo became a sunflower, and Adonis, from whose blood the anemone was created. In addition, since the early Middle Ages, flowers have held (and some still hold today) symbolic meaning. From the well-named forget-me-not to the lily of the valley (considered a good-luck charm in French tradition), none, however, has had greater conscious and unconscious associations than the rose.

Folklorists and floriculturists have been able to give numerous explanations for the supremacy of the rose in the floral kingdom, but it was artists and writers who immortalized its perfection and symbolism. Very quickly, indeed, the rose came to be equated with passionate love (red) or with platonic and pure love (white); later, in the rose-young woman parallel, it connoted her tragically short life: see, for instance, Malherbe's "Et rose elle a vécu ce que vivent les roses, / L'espace d'un matin." Of course, flowers had also been used to underline human fragility and mortality, whether in Hsüeh T'ao's "Daily the wind-flowers age, and so do I," in Robert Herrick's "daffodils," or in Sor Juana Inés de la Cruz's "All is a vain, careful device of dress, / It is a slender flower in the gale." And finally, while some writers found in the rose's thorns justifications for their pessimism, others saw that among the very same thorns blooms a magnificent flower. The most optimistic poets are those who in the spring marvel at the rebirth of the natural world and of happy life:

Yü Hsüan-chi (9th century), Charles d'Orléans, Mary Ellen Solt, whose concrete calligram, "Forsythia" (1966), is wonderfully whimsical and clever.

Robert Fleissner presents in his florilegium more than an excellent survey of the symbolism and imagery of the rose and its derivative, the poppy, sometimes also called the rose of love. In fact, the rose is here but a pretext for a persuasive and often witty discussion of nature, floral and nonfloral, as Fleissner analyzes other flowers and herbs, both medicinal and culinary, as well. And this leads him to think that, if only protagonists had a better knowledge of the sense and power of flowers and herbs, outcomes may perhaps be different. . . .

Valentine, in the opening lines of *The Two Gentlemen of Verona*, axiomatically declares, "Home-keeping youth have ever homely wits." Fleissner cannot be accused of such narrow provincialism, however, as he explores various horticultural motifs not only in works as diverse as *Romeo and Juliet*, "Kubla Khan," and *Of Human Bondage*, but also in popular culture creations like "The Naval Treaty," *The Name of the Rose*, and even that masterpiece of American film, *Citizen Kane*. Furthermore, all this is written with humor—verbal and visual—in an unpedantic, though scholarly and erudite, style. What emerges, then, are cogently argued interpretations which, when leisurely read as a whole, provide a "comparative" study that, from Shakespeare to Eco, spans almost four centuries.

Obviously, I enjoyed reading the essays comprising *A Rose by Another Name* as much as Robert Fleissner enjoyed composing them. "Beauty," he writes somewhere, "is its own justification." What better way than to consider the rose and all her sisters in one subtly fragrant garland?

Pierre L. Horn
Wright State University

Part I

Shakespeare, Roses, and the Like

"praise the deepe vermillion in the Rose"
—Sonnet 98, l. 10

"What is fairer than a rose?
What is sweeter? yet it purgeth"
—George Herbert, "The Rose"

Part I

Shakespeare, Robots, and the Like

In the first chapter, let us leave the natural world of roses *per se* to consider their preternatural significance. Although Rosalind may seem to many to represent the essence of what has later been put under the rubric of *la belle Nature*—being clean, wholesome, vivacious, lovable (even when at times feigning an anti-romantic attitude) in her free-wheeling way—certain memorable passages in *As You Like It* make her symbolic of something greater than the material world and all it represents, turning her Arden setting almost into a prelapsarian Eden. She is dubbed "heavenly" and highly lauded, to the extent that she is seemingly put in the play almost on a subliminal, symbol level with Mary. As such, she reverberates with "echoes" of the "Old Faith" (namely, Roman Catholicism) rampant in the comedy, although by no means only that denomination. For Anglicanism, too, subscribed to Christ's mother's virginity, revering St. Mary, and even as Queen Elizabeth I was adulated as Virgin Queen (whether *demi-vierge* or not). In this connection, although it is oftentimes said that true roses are not cited biblically, references in the Apocrypha, at least, would include the familiar injunction "Let us crown ourselves with rosebuds" (*Wisdom of Solomon*, 2. 8). The so-called "rose of Sharon" (*Song of Solomon*, 2. 1) is not in the Hebrew text and unrelated. But worth comparing is the King James translation of Isaiah 35. 1: "The desert shall rejoice and blossom as the rose."

It would seem as if Shakespeare's mother, at least reared as a fervent believer in the mystical rose of Mother Mary, as is commonly recognized, had a certain striking effect upon his early patterning; so let us weigh this view subtextually and in close detail. One important matter on which the lady Rosalind advises onlookers in her Epilogue is that the title of the comedy, *As You Like It*, is not merely "throw-away"; she tells them to like only "as much of this Play, as please you" (ll. 12–13).[1] As I already pointed out in correspondence in the *Times Literary Supplement*,[2] her phrase "as please you" thus rounds out the comedy thematically and in terms of its title, harking back to the original, low-keyed effect of the name we know it by. For,

3

however casual the title may appear to be, it should never be semantically correlated with an off-hand, throw-away subtitle like *What You Will* (that for *Twelfth Night*), one which in itself should actually be interpreted as relating to what the dramatist was after. It implies *What You Would Have From Will* and not simply *Do As Ye List*. Hence in his use of symbolic imagery in his early plays, Shakespeare has duly prepared the way for A ROSE BY ANOTHER NAME and not thus merely through the over-used textual allusion in *Romeo and Juliet*. That masterpiece, however, still deserves some treatment next on its own.

Although assuredly many readers would want to relate literary roses first and foremost to Juliet's all-too-familiar declaration, "That which we call a Rose, / By any other word would smell as sweete" (*Romeo and Juliet*, 2.2.43–44),[3] the vegetative imagery in her youthful tragedy actually centers more basically around herbs than flowers, which, let us say, adorn *The Winter's Tale* (4.4.98–135) rather more profusely. In thinking of herbalist imagery in the tragedy, we first of all discern the leading friar at work with his basket of simples. True, some adverse critics would insist on calling these herbs not only sweet-smelling and Nature's remedies, but as likewise partly "balefull weedes" (2.3.8). For even though Friar Laurence is warm-hearted enough, his function as a bonafide spiritual counsellor is at times open to question. The thesis here is that the drama may be better grasped in herbalistic terms than without a running metaphor to go by, the various natural properties aiding and abetting both the pros and cons of the tragic situation. Thus, one of the key herbs happens to be rosemary, which most likely is to be seen as etymologically derivative from the plant known as *ros marinus* (dew-of-the-sea), not so much from, as has also been thought, a pious reference to Christ's mother as Mystical Rose (although that association may be germane enough as well).[4]

In any event, let us depart from our rose focus as such in order to focus on related botanical kin. Whether such a transplant will convince readers other than those already set on implanting another Shakespearean rose garden in their own festive fancies is at least a challenge. Doubtless rather more is finally involved in this plot than its herbal properties, however delightfully aromatic (and at times sinister) their import: the struggle between the feuding families, love-and-death seen as a pre-Baroque leitmotif encompassed by love-and-hate and in dramatically oxymoronic fashion ("O brawling love!

O loving hate!"), a lack of moderation resulting from youthful excess and improper (although well-meant) indoctrination, or lack of it, and the overall theme of Fate versus Voluntarism in the final determination of this star-crossed tragedy. For example, does Romeo merely "deny" or go as far as actually to "defy" his "stars"? The texts tell different tales. How, then, might we not inquire, would herbal lore correlate such major issues? The answer is that, as with all of Shakespeare's works, the ultimate complexity is to be arrived at from a myriad of minor factors. Clearly one major problem that can hardly be shunted aside is the extent to which what has been called natural law applies and how it can here be accommodated. The use of herb imagery relates both to such law and to the human organism considered as the Temple of the Holy Spirit. As a long-time devotee of proper nutrition, I submit that the lowly herb indeed has its place representing yet again a rose by another name.

Notes

1. References to Shakespeare throughout are to *William Shakespeare: The Complete Works*, gen. ed. Alfred Harbage (Baltimore: Penguin, 1969), with old spelling and punctuation from *The First Folio of Shakespeare*, prepared by Charlton Hinman (New York: Norton, 1968).

2. Letter to the Editor of the *TLS*, 24 May 1985, p. 579.

3. In this instance, the more familiar reading is "By any other *name* would smell as sweet," but the Pelican notations indicate that "word" is already found in the Second Quarto and thus may be the correct or intended reading.

4. See Ch. I. Thus, the rosemary "was in early use in England as a Christmas flower recalling the Nativity of Christ." See Eva C. Haugen, *Symbols, Our Universal Language* (Wichita: McCormick-Armstrong, 1962), p. 216.

Chapter I

As You Like *Rosa*lind;
or,
"Arden and ... Merry" / Mary Arden:
Calling on Shakespeare's Mother
in *As You Like It*

It is frequently maintained that the Forest of *Arden* in *As You Like It* represents not only the Anglicized form of the French *Ardennes*, but cannot help "echoing" the maiden name of Shakespeare's at least one-time Catholic mother, Mary Arden.[1] Because stage tradition informs us that the dramatist took the role of the prelapsarian Adam in the theater—as well as, perhaps, that of William (they do not appear concomitantly)[2]—he may indeed have assumed, whether consciously or not, a private interest in this comedy's intriguing topical allusions. It is also likely enough, given his penchant for meaningful name play here and elsewhere, that he incorporated subtle paronomasia on his mother's original *full* name—*Mary* along with *Arden*. If so, such a promising new lead regarding his use of his family nomenclature would serve not only to rebuff once again the anti-Stratfordians, those die-hard "heretics" who persist in believing the plays were composed by the Earl of Oxford, or Lord Bacon, but would relate aesthetically in what this drama is all about, in short to its moral message.

Such crucial name play operates in the very first scene when Charles says of Duke Senior, "hee is already in the Forrest of *Arden*, and a many *merry* men with him" (1.1.107–8).[3] In terms of the more obvious immediate context, the reference is matter-of-factly to "Robin Hood and his merry men"—an allusion which is again clearly instrumental, incidentally, in projecting an English proper name, or resonance thereof, upon an originally French setting (the *Ardennes*), thereby allowing for a new connotative signification which provides a further topical effect. In brief, it provides for a subliminal reverberation of the playwright's mother's name: Mary Arden Shakespeare. The maternal effect is at least comfortable.

At this poignant juncture, we may fancy some skeptical reader nonchalantly shrugging and quibbling, "But what has that to do with *the play?*" In a similar, even more discomfiting manner, another cynical critic might try to disarm us with an aside like this: "Since the play, after all, is called *As You Like It* ... why not?" The question, then, is whether the problem of an implicit autobiographical "echo" is of truly significant enough import to deserve to waylay the unsuspecting reader. If it is, clearly any valid new insight into Shakespeare's background deserves the most careful scrutiny. After all, if only a Robin Hood reference was intended, the setting would better have been Sherwood Forest rather than that of Arden.

My initial response to such hypothetical demurrers as those briefly posed above is that they are entirely ungermane to my basic purpose, which concerns itself with the play as a historical *document*, one embedding a script but also revelatory, perforce, of its author. Thus my fundamental approach is not so much with "speech play" as with what we would now designate "text play." The question finally of whether or not an audience would have been captivated enough by such a hidden play on words, whether or not it is "justified" by the seemingly off-hand nature of the title, or whether or not it is structurally significant, is somewhat beside the point. For the text of a drama, like that of any other written literary composition, is historically, first and foremost, a document providing clues about its "occasion." Only secondarily may it be said to "live a life of its own" as an artifact, one relatively independent of its author. As T.S. Eliot himself once cryptically stated, in his famous essay "Hamlet and His Problems," "*Qua* work of art, the work of art cannot be interpreted: there is nothing to interpret...." Sobeit.

My proposal therefore is that the close conjunction of the words "*Arden*" (italicized, for what it is worth, in the Folio text) and "merry" is not only elementary, but striking enough to intimate some kind of subliminal kinship. Already on the overt level elsewhere, *As You Like It* exhibits a goodly share of the wordplay of England's wittiest poet—a point that would support our case.

Chapter I: As You Like Rosalind

For, drawing upon an analogous enough autobiographical allusion, we might enlist the recent remarkable revelation by Andrew Gurr that the seemingly isolated phrase "hate away" in Sonnet 145 obliquely alludes as well to the Shakespeare family, specifically even to another female member thereof, namely the dramatist's spouse, formerly Anne *Hathaway*. The terms have at least a blurred resemblance. The familiar jinglet comes to mind: "Whoever hath her will, Anne hath a way"; or as James Joyce put it in *Ulysses*, "If others have their will Ann hath a way." Textually speaking, moreover, in line nine of this sonnet, the conjunction of *hate* and *an* in close proximity (*"hate* ... altered with *an"*) is instructive because it implies a meaning additional to the obvious surface one. Since *"an"* invites further submerged paronomasia (on *Anne*), emerging as a hidden variant of the name, we find that *"hate"* in effect is indeed literally "altered with *an"* even in more ways than one. Not only does the alteration suggest wordplay on the name in general, but the order of the name allusions is itself altered or reversed: the wordplay on the surname precedes that on the Christian name. The significance of this reading, here, is that precisely the same kind of submerged name play in reverse manifests itself in the hitherto overlooked passage on *Arden* and *merry* in *As You Like It*.

Another analogy of more than passing interest to the philologist is the fairly unrestrained text play on the homonym *Marry* somewhat earlier in the first scene. After Oliver petulantly inquires, "What *mar* you then sir?" Orlando casually responds, *"Marry* sir, I am helping you to *mar* that which God made" (1.1.29–30).[4] The resonances of *Marry* are worth examining here: they denote not only the common expletive (or mild ejaculation), but the concepts of both *wedding* and being *merry*. Further, they invite hidden allusions, let us say, to *Mary*, including wordplay on the first three letters: M-a-r. Agreed, it could be contended that such subtlety would not come across readily on the stage, but that is really beside the textual point when we are examining orthographic and not homophonic punning. True, too, many of Shakespeare's examples of wordplay did depend on homophony or near homophony, but only theater-manic, specialized people might insist that what he wrote needs to be understood solely in terms of the proscenium arch. If we turn from text to performance, we stray away from contemplation of essence and toward only an evaluation of a limited manifestation of that essence. What presumably the playwright consciously or unconsciously intended has to be of primary import—difficult though that sometimes may be to decipher.

We notice next that the phrase "*mar* that which God made": promotes additional, ludic wordplay on religious matters, though not, I should infer, in any irreverent sense. The likelihood that orthographic punning on "mar" was deliberate is seen from the very manner in which Orlando's statement serves to anticipate the well-recognized wordplay on Sir Oliver *Mar*-text's name to ensue. The *mar / Marry* quibbling, moreover, is set within the spirited context of further witticism: only compare, for example, the clear-cut punning on *Nothing* and *naught* (1.1.17, 32)—hardly raucous humor by modern-day standards, but acceptable enough then.

In terms of its *immediate* context, "Marry," to be sure, represents little more than a mild ejaculation derivative of the mild oath "By the Virgin Mary"; in terms of its larger, *mediate* context, however (to appropriate a distinction gleaned from biblical hermeneutics), it peers straight ahead thematically to the four-fold marrying at the end. Thereby it relates to the drama structurally. In a still deeper, psychological as well as theological, sense, then, the interconnection between "Mary" and both the Virgin and the dramatist's mother's name specifically and pointedly is proleptic of the implicit biographical wordplay on the *Arden / Merry* cluster to follow.

In this respect, regarding the relation between uncomic wit and religion, curiously enough one can hardly help recollecting that the most famous work of medieval times is known in English translation as *The Divine Comedy*. True, the Italian term *Commedia* had a different meaning, but that is ungermane to our purposes here. It has been common knowledge, then presumably as today, that the Roman Church credits itself for having been founded, in point of linguistic fact, upon uncomic wordplay. "Thou art Peter, and upon this rock I shall build my church" (*Matt.* 16.18) implies name play on *petra*, meaning *rock* in both Greek and Aramaic, as well as Armenian, Coptic, Persian, and Ethiopian—a pun, incidentally, documented not by theologians alone but by literary critics (such as Meyer H. Abrams in his standard workbook, *A Glossary of Literary Terms*).[5] With such a precedent before us, would tasteful Mariological punning seem necessarily inappropriate or irreverent? Most likely not, we might think, at least so long as it did not become, let us say, Mariol*atrous*. For what it is worth, the Church of England, to which Shakespeare has been said to have gravitated more in his later years, as the style

Chapter I: As You Like Rosalind

of his will for instance reveals, traditionally has venerated St. Mary, too, as in the naming of its church architecture.

What is the real aesthetic significance of the name play? It points, let us imagine, to a "Marian" theme operative in the drama, one that runs throughout it like a kind of *Leitmotif.* To begin, Rosalind, we recall, is termed "heavenly" and as having "all graces," even as the Virgin was "full of grace." Rosalind's very name would evoke that of Mary as the Mystical Rose—along with the usual rosary associations. We recall also the crowning of the *rosière* in France, the lady of good virtue or "daughter of Mary" harking back to c. 535 (hence a Mystical Rose association even before Dante). Nature granted mankind a boon with Rosalind, Shakespeare informs us, and Wordsworth's now-familiar descriptive phrase "our tainted nature's solitary boast," applicable to Mary as being born without Original Sin, according to Catholic doctrine, easily comes to mind. Let us hasten to add that, by such an inference, we hardly mean to imply that the Stratford bard was "previewing" the dogma of the Immaculate Conception. What we may wish respectfully to propose is that cognizance of *our* primal sin, that of fallen mankind, does run through the play thematically with its overt hints of both prelapsarian bliss and postlapsarian after-effects. For instance, the name of *Arden*, as is generally admitted, acts in aesthetic counterpoint to the meaning of *Eden*. That very contrast hardly detracts from the proposed autobiographical connection, however, but rather serves to underscore whatever religious import it may have. Duke Senior specifically reminds us that visitors are not to feel in Arden "the penaltie of *Adam*" (2.1.5), meaning the overall effect that primal sin has had on nature as a whole (evident, for example, in reference to the "seasons difference" a few lines later, a concept which Milton then built upon, as is well recognized, in *Paradise Lost*). No tornadoes, hurricanes, or vile earthquakes existed before the Fall. This view makes more sense, at any rate, than the inference that Shakespeare was indulging in subliminal back-to-the-womb longings in naming his paradise *Arden.* For, as we have seen, the figure of Adam (sometimes thought to have been played by Shakespeare) is present too. Certainly the line "He dies that touches any of this fruite" (2.7.98) was meant to summon to our receptive minds the Old Testament tale of fruit forbidden.

Yet, at the same time, *As You Like It* is clearly also set in a New Testament, *post*lapsarian century. Indeed, the very generic concept of comedy (as derivative of *commedia*) embodies the theme of a shift from sin to salvation. René E. Fortin, in a helpful account of religious imagery in this play,[6] designated Orlando a Christ-figure since he is paralleled with Hercules, a type of the Savior (1.2.192), and saves Oliver from a beast reminiscent of that overthrown by Hercules as well as from a snake, both animals incidentally recalling Psalm 91.13. Orlando then delivers Oliver from moral evil. Although some Shakespeareans are reluctant to apply the critical term "Christ-figure," Fortin's deft analysis deserves scrutiny. Oliver's spontaneous conversion to love is deemed appropriately a "mystery of grace," for he is enamored of Celia, whose name originally stands for *heaven*. The drama, nonetheless, reflects, in addition, the classical concept of the Golden Age, even if ironically at times.

Should the query be raised whether Rosalind is truly or intrinsically reflective of ideals embodied in Mary, consider the following evidence. To arrive at a proper response based on Marian research (to submit to the leading Marian annual), I visited purportedly the world's largest repository of Marian materials at the University of Dayton Library in Ohio. Although I was unsuccessful in uncovering any relevant document or comment from Elizabethan times which would shed light on more Mariological punning, I did come upon some criticism, which has some validity not only as a Roman view but one catholic in a larger sense. I discovered that Sister Mary Julian Baird, R.S.M., originally writing for the now-defunct journal *Sacred Heart Messenger*, lauded Shakespeare's heroine as follows: "There is another girl in the early comedies who exhibits Our Lady's virtues in a vivid way—Rosalind in *As You Like It*. Her joyous nature is full of fun: she is kind and loyal and loving. So must Mary of Nazareth have been." A simple-hearted, pious comment this, yet one also fairly instructive with regard to Shakespeare from a practical point of view. The copy of her article which I located was reprinted in a journal devoted to Mary, the essay itself being simply but beautifully entitled "Shakespeare and Our Lady."[7] I thereby first felt it almost *de rigueur* to entitle my own research "As You Like Our Lady"—cavalier though such a designation may appear to certain Shakespeareans. Perhaps "As You Like *Rosa*lind" is ecumenically more apropos.

Another bit of research ought also to be recounted, this time more experiential, first-hand, and "theater-wise" than theological or theoretical. During the summer of 1978, I had the opportunity to witness a commendable production of the comedy by a local group in Oxford, England, directed by Arthur Kincaid and produced in a central Catholic church. Most striking was the simplicity of the production as highlighted by the natural appeal of Rosalind, a buoyant "nature girl" in more ways than one, being un-made-up and barefoot on the intimate, improvised stage. Her overall graces were such as to support the familiar ecclesiastical dictum that "the supernatural builds upon the natural," heavenly grace thereby building on bodily grace. It is hard therefore not to imagine that an attentive audience would be aware of submerged wordplay in the key *Arden / merry* passage at the very beginning—subtle though admittedly it is—as strengthening the redemptive effect she has for the theatergoer as well as the regular scholar in his study. True, Rosalind is represented as noticeably *more* realistic than romantic, but such a label would scarcely be opposed to the standard view espoused by church tradition that, as St. Thomas Aquinas put it in a key phrase, nothing is in the mind which is not first in the (external) senses.

Finally the submerged punning on Mary's name sheds further light on Shakespeare's penchant for name play in his later, more mature dramas. How deliberate such wordplay was is, again, an open question, one not necessarily relevant. When he invented the name of Falstaff, for instance, he surely would have indulged somehow in implicit punning on his own name (in that, to cite the old chestnut, when a spear shakes, it follows that the staff falls), and he has been said to have his son, named *Hamnet* (a common variant of *Hamlet*) partially in the back of his mind when he composed his Danish tragedy (for the son had recently died). —Yet how far should such an analogy be accepted? Legend has it also that Shakespeare played the part of the ghost, who was thereby the Prince's father in more ways than one. Commenting on James Joyce's use of this legendry, Martin Scofield criticizes: "We can hardly take this seriously. . . ." Yet he then makes a subtle qualification: "Stephen himself does not seem to take his ideas seriously, or at least, he does not *believe* in his theory."[8] The question is why, then, does he entertain such a thought in the first place? More seems to be involved than teasing the reader. —Might not Joyce have been more intuitive here than speculative?

Bearing in mind the necessary caveats, we may concur that although Jesus's mother might be reverently thought of even, let us say, as a "prelapsarian person extant in postlapsarian times," we would go a bit far in pursuing the Marian "identification" with Rosalind in every respect. For one thing, she excites, in passing at least, concupiscent desires (3.2.107). But was not Mary herself true woman as well as the greatest saint? As an abstraction, sexuality, it has been said, *is* Woman. That such an association would not necessarily detract from a Marian reading can be admitted if we compare the historical congruence of devotions to the Virgin in the medieval period with the emergence of the so-called courtly love tradition with some of its notorious excesses in response to the mechanical *mariage de convenance*, the most prominent being the adulterous love between Lancelot and Guinevere. In both cases, at any rate, *obedience to the lady* constituted the ideal, whether that lady turned out to be "Our Lady" or was, say, another married spouse. In any event, the passing temptation of lust is hardly as memorable, from an aesthetically contemplative standpoint, as what Sister Mary Julian refers to as "the joy of Rosalind," thereby recounting Marian pleasures associated with those of the rosary, namely its Joyful Mysteries. From this point of view, Rosalind deserves a *critical* Novena.[9] *Ad maiorem gloriam Dei.*

It might also be finally pointed out how, although it is generally admitted that there need be no intrinsic connection between name and thing (see Chapter XIV), man continually seeks for some kind of magical identification. In some cases, a conjectured connotative association seems unwarrantedly absurd, however, such as believing that an anticipation of *hell* as the Moor's tragic destiny has to be present in Othello's very name. Such a perverse reading would be tantamount to trying to limit the powers of God. The case for a Marian Rose operative in *Rosalind* is somewhat better, let us pray.[10]

Notes

1. See, e.g., Harry Levin, "Shakespeare's Nomenclature," in *Essays on Shakespeare*, ed. Gerald W. Chapman (Princeton: Princeton University Press, 1965), pp. 59–90 (especially 76); rpt. in Levin, *Shakespeare and the Revolution of the Times* (New York: Oxford University Press, 1976). See also Murray J. Levith, *What's in Shakespeare's Names* (Hamden, Ct.: Archon Books, 1978) and the special "Names in Shakespeare" issue of *Names* (American Name Society), 35 (1987).

Chapter I: As You Like Rosalind

2. See William M. Jones, "William Shakespeare as William in *As You Like It*," *Shakespeare Quarterly*, 11 (1960), 228–31. Further supportive of the view that Shakespeare could have doubled as Arden and William is Stephen Booth's "Speculations on Doubling in Shakespeare's Plays," in *Shakespeare: The Theatrical Dimension*, ed. Philip E. McGuire and David A. Samuelson (New York: AMS Press, 1979), pp. 103–31.

3. Aside from *"Arden,"* which is italicized in the First Folio, other words from Shakespeare here and elsewhere have italics added.

4. For more on the vicar Mar-text in this biographical context, see my correspondence in *Shakespeare Quarterly*, 25 (1974), 285.

5. 3rd ed. (New York: Holt, Rinehart and Winston, 1971), p. 139.

6. "'Tongues in Trees': Symbolic Patterns in *As You Like It*," *Texas Stud. in Lit. and Lang.*, 14 (1973), 568–82. Cf. Alice-Lyle Scoufos, "The *Paradiso Terrestre* and the Testing of Love in *As You Like It*," *Shakespeare Studies*, 14 (1981), 215–27. Orlando and Oliver relate to the *Song of Roland*, where, however, their roles are reversed. (I owe this point to Pierre L. Horn of Wright State University, who was kind enough to read through this entire book in manuscript form and make valuable suggestions.)

7. *Our Lady's Digest* (Twin Lakes, Wisconsin), 17 (1963), 325–31.

8. *The Ghosts of Hamlet: The Play and Modern Writers* (Cambridge: Cambridge University Press, 1980), p. 62.

9. Eric Poole, in "The Ancestors of Mary Arden," *Shakespeare Newsletter*, 31 (Sept./Nov. 1981), 30, has found new information relating the name *Rosalind* to that of Shakespeare's mother. He discussed the commonly recognized main source, Thomas Lodge's *Rosalynde*, pointing to what "is certainly the earliest document certainly relating to ancestors of Shakespeare" (from the year 1501).

10. For more on a Catholic Rosalind that came to my attention only at the last moment, see F. W. Brownlow, "John Shakespeare's Recusancy: New Light on an Old Document," *Shakespeare Quarterly*, 40 (1989), 186–91 (especially 190).

Chapter II

Rosemary in *Romeo and Juliet* and Other Herbs

> "Nasti mulam anausadham ...
> yojakastatra durlabhah"
> (There is no herb that is not a
> medicine ... what is rare is the
> man who knows how to put it to
> right use)
> —Sanskrit saying

> "Shakespeare had appeared more
> than once in *Ulysses* walking 'in a
> rosery of Fetter Lane of Gerard,
> herbalist'"
> —Barbara Seward,
> *The Symbolic Rose*

Even as, in Shakespeare's day, herb cultivation was in vogue, we have good rationale for tracing significant allusions to medicinal, aromatic, and even deviously poisonous characteristics of herbs in his dramaturgy. As a leading authority, E. S. Rohde, has remarked, "more herbs figure in Shakespeare's writings than in those of any of his contemporaries save the herbalists"; indeed the well-scented plays include "over twenty herbs exclusive of various garden flowers valued as much for their herbal properties as for their beauty."[1] Shakespearean flora in general have been similarly cultivated.[2] Hence still another dedicated study of his dramatic vegetation, stressing herbaceous shrubbery, should also prove of nascent value. Let us commence, then, by concentrating on *Romeo and Juliet*, in some key respects a veritable "herb play," taking into useful, passing account other important herbal allusions in the dramas when need be.

I

To begin, herbs were considered much in line with ordinary flowers (thus linking again with my title), for simples "as we know them now, were planted indiscriminately with flowers,"[3] thereby incidentally helping to buttress the present inclusion. It is quite possible that Shakespeare had visited the gardens of Kenilworth and was familiar with far more than his native gardens at Stratford-upon-Avon. He could likewise have seen such a treatise as *Maison Rustique, or Countrie Farme*, of Charles Stevens and John Leebault, Doctors of Physicke,[4] if we would enlist a horticultural contrast. In any event, like all Englishmen, he certainly knew how dear to their hearts was the traditional *hortus conclusus* (enclosed garden), which became a vital metaphor stemming from medieval times and enrichening the Renaissance. Consult, for example, a well-known treatise like Alicia Amherst's *A History of Gardening in England*[5] or Edward Hyams's more recent *The English Garden*.[6] On Elizabethan herbaria in particular, Ellen Eyler's *Early English Gardens and Garden Books*[7] is especially compact, useful, and accessible. Two valuable studies of Shakespeare's garden lore are Frederick G. Savage's *The Flora and Folk Lore of Shakespeare*[8] and the work by Rohde, but others abound, including Mats Rydén's *Shakespearean Plant Names: Identifications and Interpretations*.[9] Common herbs used for purposes medicinal are the subject of W. Coles's *The Art of Simpling: An Introduction to the Knowledge and Gathering of Plants*; although published as late as 1656 in London, it has been reprinted as a handy vade mecum for understanding flora in the dramatist's own time.[10] A variety of other such products of Elizabethan study and vintage can be profitably consulted.[11] To round off the vegetative picture, as for the famous mulberry tree story, for what that may be worth here, devotees have a useful tool; the tale was revived during the four-hundredth anniversary of Shakespeare's birth and is considered in detail in Christian Deelman's *The Great Shakespeare Jubilee*.[12]

As for herbal effects in the star-crossed tragedy itself, first of all let us consider ten herbs not cited in this "herb tragedy," for it is helpful enough to commence with the rhetorical device of arousing interest by telling what something is *not* before centering on what it

Chapter II: Rosemary in Romeo and Juliet and Other Herbs

finally *must be*. At any rate, these ten also enter the tragedy through its back yard: hyssop, balm, marjoram, lavender, thyme, fumitory, camomile, mint, holy thistle, and aloe. Let us now survey some of the typical usages along with their subliminal meanings.

In *Othello*, two come together: "Sow lettuce, set hyssop and weed up thyme" (1.3.325). *Hyssop* was often "set" (or planted) in the form of a maze, illustrations of which are to be found in plates at the end of the Eyler pamphlet. Its acerbic quality gives it special poignancy for this pathetic tragedy. As an herb applicable for purification purposes, it has been used to clean temples and similar edifices; "water of hyssop" obtained in ritualistic sprinkling. An overtone of this purpose is in the plays, indirectly in the Moor's having been baptized (2.3.326), his reverting to a pre-Christian form of justice at the end notwithstanding. Hence we might go further and contend that he was *only* "ritualistically" affected, not truly spiritually. Although baptismal rites, like baths of purification in other religions, did not absolutely require hyssop water, still the connotation of water used for purification purposes is subtextually present.

Thyme, too, was noted for its medicinal properties; according to Parkinson, in his *Paradisus*, it had its special value for the melancholic. Various victims of such dramatized melancholia include Antipholus of Syracuse in *The Comedy of Errors*, Antonio in *The Merchant of Venice* (whose initial problem some overly venturesome critics have ascribed to homosexuality, but it may respond to a simpler, nature cure), Jaques in *As You Like It*, to some extent Sir John Falstaff (who has the humour of melancholy because he laments growing old and becomes extremely distraught over being demoted when Hal becomes king), and above all Prince Hamlet, not to mention those who, in their various melancholy ways, adumbrate him, like Richard II and Brutus.

Balm, also designated balsam or balsamum, has a sweet scent and had been traditionally employed by knights for healing wounds. Planted at the Shakespeare House in Stratford-upon-Avon, in the celebrated gardens, it bursts forth also in *The Merry Wives of Windsor* as the "juice of balm" (5.5.60). Its use in the anointing of monarchs is cited in *3 Henry VI* (3.1.17), *Troilus and Cressida* (1.1.58), *The Comedy of Errors* (4.1.89), and *Macbeth* (2.2.38). Because one particular ecclesiastical use of balm was in the form of Zakkum, known as *Balanites aegyptiaca*, the Balm of Gilead, anagogic connotations may enter in again, dramatically, as well.

Turning next to *marjoram*, also called ditanny, we discern familiar mention made in Sonnet 99: "And buds of marjerom had stolne thy haire" (l. 7). This herbal allusion has provoked much comment, notably the question of whether a youth or lady (or allowably even a lady-like youth) was being described. The simple is cited elsewhere with approbation, even reverence. In *The Winter's Tale*, we hear of "Hot Lavender, Mints, Savory, Marjorum" (4.4.104); in *King Lear*, it becomes a shibboleth: "Give the word. —Sweet Marjorum. —Passe. —I know that voice" (4.6.92–95); in *All's Well*, we hear of "the sweete Margerom of the sallet, or rather, the hearbe of grace" (4.5.14–15). Rohde relates marjoram as the herb-of-grace to religious repentance, noting that "Loudon writing in 1838 says rue 'is to this day called Ave Grace in Sussex.'"[13] No wonder monks trafficked religiously in herbal culture.

Fumitory, in *Henry V* ("her fallow Leas [the Darnell, Hemlock, and ranke Femetary] / Doth root upon"—5.2.44–46), has been taken as one of the wild meadow herbs (which poor demented Lear twisted around his neck for a garland taking the place of his crown). One of the delicate herbs, fumitory gets its name from its grayish appearance, suggesting "smoke of the earth." In similar guise, "much-trodden *camomile*," so called because of *1 Henry IV* ("the more it is troden [on], the faster it growes"—2.4.382–83), was designated the Earth Apple because of its pomaceous odor. Another herb of healing powers,[14] it was especially wholesome in tea.

Mint, which is cited signally in *Love's Labour's Lost* ("I am that flower. —That mint. —That columbine"—5.2.647–8) and in *The Winter's Tale* (as noted above), was familiar already to Chaucer and even earlier to Pliny. It, too, has received a special religious significance. Holmesworthe, for instance, remarks that "one very old use of mint is still retained in Holstein, Germany, where, when the peasants attend a funeral, they often carry bunches of it in their hands."[15] Another herb with a pleasant enough scent was *lavender* (also cited in *The Winter's Tale*). Etymologically related to *lavendre*, from which we derive the term *laundress*, it has, as might be expected, an especially clean, salutary smell, one suggestive of purification.

Holy thistle had its curious properties. Holmesworth notes: "The holy thistle, or blessed thistle as it is sometimes called, although not

Chapter II: Rosemary in Romeo and Juliet and Other Herbs

often seen now, was, at the period Shakespeare lived, much thought of by the old country folk. It held a high reputation for its healing propensities. It was said to cure forgetfulness and be even good in curing the plague, in some instances."[16] We shall briefly consider the relevance of this herb to *Romeo and Juliet*, even as the Black Death heralds its tragic outcome.

Lastly, *aloe*, referred to in a work oftentimes taken as Shakespeare's (even as it was published with his *Sonnets*), notably *A Lover's Complaint*, ll. 272–3, "... sweetens in the suffring pangues it beares, / The *Alloes* of all forces, shockes and feares" and was recognized as an herb of the most intense bitterness. It is traceable to Dioscorides, who provided careful instructions for its employment. Prepared as a purgative during Shakespeare's time, the leading Renaissance herbalist, John Gerard, mentions it in his *Herbal* of 1597. (For a comprehensive account of the various herbals during this period, consult the selective bibliography appended.)

Having now considered herbs *not* mentioned in the "herbal play" of *Romeo and Juliet*, let us examine those in it as well with the hope of coming to valid conclusions regarding the value of such herbalist study even with reference to a noted Shakespearean tragedy.

II

Three major herbs in the star-crossed tragedy are *rosemary, wormwood,* and *plantain*; we consider them now in turn, the most noteworthy for our purposes first. Other herbs we may find germane to the play, too, if not so directly, as we shall see.

Three references to the popular Elizabethan simple rosemary are worthy of immediate pause: "Doth not Rosemarie and *Romeo* begin both with a letter?" (2.4.219) (obviously so, but it may be the sound rather than the letter *per se* which counts); "Drie up your teares, and sticke your Rosemarie / On this faire Coarse, and as the custome is, / And in her best array beare her to Church: / For though some Nature bids all us lament, / Yet Natures teares are Reasons merriment" (4.5.79–83). The notable recommendation of this herb was that it could strengthen the memory. Thus Ovid: "Rosemarie comforteth the brayne, and restoreth speech; especially the conserve made of the flowers thereof with sugar" (*Metamorphoses*,

XII.409). Newton, in his biblical herbal, claimed that rosemary "cheereth both the heart and mind of man"; Turner, in his *Newe Herball* (1551), referred to "rosa-mary" as put in medicines. In its alleviating melancholia, it was allied to thyme. Grindon wrote: "In the suave little poem, 'a Nosegay alwaies sweet, for Lovers,' in the 'Handefull of Pleasant Delites,' ... we have—

> Rosemarie is for remembrance
> Betweene us daie and night,
> Wishing that I might alwaies have
> You present in my sight.

Can we wonder that it was consecrated to friendship...? It was introduced ... among the symbols used at funerals, as in *Romeo and Juliet* ... and in the spirit of the gold ring, emblem of constancy, among those used also at weddings, when a sprig of rosemary was put in the wine dedicated especially to good wishes for the bride's happiness."[17] Rosemary was an herb with a rich variety of uses—not even to mention cooking.

Curiously, a question arises about the origin of the herb's name, for Turner's allusion to it as "rosa-mary" appears etymologically inexact: it derives not from combining *Rose* and *Mary*,[18] its being known as the Christmas herb notwithstanding, but from the Latin *ros* and *marinus*, meaning "dew of the sea." Still, it seems clear enough that Shakespeare would have been acquainted with the popular religious connotations associated with the Yuletide etymology, or at least that such awareness played its role in his tragedy. For he expected his audiences to be herbalistically sophisticated.

In search of a conclusive answer, we might bear in mind two separate accounts of the English history of this herb: (1) Rosemary was mentioned in Old English herbals and wordhoards (vocabulary lists) and so was probably already introduced, as E. S. Rohde claimed, "in Roman times, if not before";[19] (2) it was reintroduced by Philippa of Hainault, Queen of Edward III. A manuscript, now preserved in the Trinity College Library in Cambridge, England, treats of the virtues of the herb; the Countess of Hainault sent it to her daughter, Queen Philippa. Here we find many traditions concerning the herb, including the religious. Because a major part of the manuscript was incorporated in Banckes' *Herbal* in 1525, well-read Elizabethans knew of this information. For what it is worth,

Rohde goes so far as to assert unequivocally that "Shakespeare was doubtless familiar with Banckes' *Herbal.*"[20]

Still, as far as herbals in general are concerned, he more likely would have acquainted himself with the work of William Turner, the so-called father of English botany, or with John Gerard's familiar *Herbal; or, General History of Plants*. These works, however, do not make such a point of the religious aspects the way, for example, L. Lemnius' *An Herbal for the Bible* obviously does. Shakespeare probably did not, however, have ready access to the more abstruse studies, such as Aemilius Macer's *De naturis, qualitatibus, et virtutibus herbarum* (translated by Robert Wyer as *Macer's Herbal, Practys'd by Doctor Lynacre*).[21] Insufficient evidence supports the view that Shakespeare gave rosemary a specific religious meaning, but unquestionably it would have had that connotation for many members of his audience. In *Hamlet*, Ophelia's "There's Rosemary, that's for Remembraunce. / Pray love remember" (4.5.174–5) conveys a religious resonance beneath the surface with the key terms *Rose, Mary*, and *pray*. These words are resonant from the Ghost's last words to Hamlet, after their initial encounter, namely "remember me!" (1.5.91).[22] Although scholars have speculated whether such an almost throw-away phrase might not simply mean for Hamlet to get the job of revenge over with, or more abstrusely that the audience should recall forever that Hamlet's creator purportedly took the role of the revenant on the stage, the parallel in Ophelia's talk might well suggest that the purgatorial soul is asking for prayers. The rose symbol has further, archetypal signification, referring to the "heart" but even more to what was subtly called the "mystic centre" in man, and some of these overtones could latently have worked their way into the overall meaning of *rosemary* in the drama.

Next, *wormwood*, cited in the star-crossed tragedy twice, has considerable herbal resonance. The Nurse says candidly, "I had then laid Worme-wood to my Dug" (1.3.26), referring again to "the Worme-wood on the nipple of my Dugge" (30–1) which was "bitter" (31); the clear implication was that the herb was used for weaning, thereby reflecting on the earthy character of Juliet's wet-nurse. Reverting to *Hamlet*, we find the connotation of bitterness in the Prince's exclamation of "Wormwood, Wormwood" (3.2.173). (In some versions, his phrase is "That's wormwood.") Although it might seem to be to envision similarities between these two tragedies in their mutual use of two principal herbs, rosemary and wormwood, a few major parallels augment such relationships. Let us see how.

Aside from the religious quandaries, both dramas exhibit strong puzzlement over the question of fate versus free will. Whereas Romeo does not know whether or not to "deny" or "defy" his stars (5.1.24)—depending upon which text the reader chooses—Hamlet bides his time after his return from the trip to England ostensibly so fate can run its course (as in 5.2.73–4) but also plausibly because of a weakness in his makeup. Psychologically, both heroes exhibit a strong feeling that their flesh is tainted. Romeo specifies "this world-wearied flesh" (5.3.112) as if anticipating the Prince's famous soliloquy commencing, as the First Folio text has it, "O, that this too too solid flesh, would melt, / Thaw, and resolve it selfe into a Dew" (1.2.129–30). In this case, however, the textual crux is in the later, Danish tragedy, most scholars today reading "sullied" (or even "sallied"), not "solid," an emphasis upon sordidness which even more closely relates to Romeo's lamentation. (It is arguable that "solid flesh" would have been comically embarrassing if an obese Burbage had to recite the line.)

One further use of wormwood is notable: it was supposedly employed to counteract the effects of the love juice in *A Midsummer Night's Dream*. Whereas Cupid's flower had put Titania to sleep, Oberon used wormwood upon her closed eyelids to wake her from the love dream. This association with love's powers gives it further significance in a love tragedy like that of Romeo and his Juliet. Its bitterness may even suggest its having a flavor that is here foreboding.

Finally, *plantain*, also called waibred and waybroad, plays a certain role in the tragedy: "Your Plantan leafe is excellent" (1.2.51). It is regimen for a broken shin. Originally discovered by the physician Themison, plantain became one of the nine sacred herbs in the eleventh-century *Lacnunga*.

So, to sum things up, three major herbs can now be found germane to this drama: one in reference to felicitude (rosemary); another, in contrast, in relation to bitterness (wormwood); lastly, one simply related to healing (plantain). Symbolically, they help to underscore three aspects of the tragedy worth contemplating: its initial happy love troth, its acrid "consumation" in death, and the final healing breach between the two feuding families. The symbols become interwoven, the deaths representing love-death, and

Chapter II: Rosemary in Romeo and Juliet and Other Herbs

allusions to healing may reflect more than one herb, even all the simples mentioned combined, or could refer to the friar's familiar herb-basket (being instrumental in bringing about the tragic union, but then also the reconciliation). In this respect, Shakespeare's herbs can have a vital thematic, textural meaning; they help to enrichen the *total* value of the dramatic imagery, providing more than a merely culinary overtone.

A few remaining herbs are also worth taking into account as possibly akin to the deeper meaning of this romantic tragedy. Because they are not alluded to specifically by name, we may only guess at what they may be. With some knowledge of Renaissance herbs at our command, however, our interpretations may be a bit more than merely random and have their calculated effect. For instance, Friar Laurence is traditionally portrayed with his basket of simples, even as the apothecary is depicted as having dispensed somewhat different herbs in the chemist's shop. In the first case, the herbs involved, save for the "balefull Weedes" alluded to, are wholesome ones; in the second, poisonous. We may quite validly conjecture that some of the salutary herbs cited in other plays are expected also in the friar's basket: marjoram, balm, lavender, thyme, fumitory, camomile, and mint. But what were the devious growths that the dreary apothecary bestowed on Romeo? Let us consider these in a little more detail.

Surely one of the poisonous herbs dispensed by the druggist may well have been *monk's hood.* Mentioned in *2 Henry IV*, 4.4.47, this plant was also known as wolf's bane. Gerard, in his famous herbal, referred to the large "yellow Swiss species."[23] Found in shady places beside streams, it was wild in Europe and available as far as the Himalaya region. Yet, although Bloom has asserted categorically that "the poison of the apothecary in *Romeo and Juliet* may be that extracted from this terribly deadly plant,"[24] it is by no means the only candidate. Let us consider a close rival: *hemlock.*

This dangerous herb appears in *Henry V*, 5.2.45, and *King Lear*, 4.4.4, and Shakespeare knew about the most famous death from the poison: Socrates'. It was likewise deemed fit for a witch's broth, mention of it being found in *Macbeth* ("Roote of Hemlocke, digg'd i' th' darke"—4.1.25). Rohde cites this eerie line as revealing how "the properties of certain plants are strongest at night,"[25] a fittingly ominous association. The perils of the deadly nightshade family come to mind. Hemlock was also the label given at times to a harmless herb, but it is doubtful that "fools' parsley" in *Lear* (4.4.4) is that. The poison of the apothecary could also have been extracted from *henbane, moonwort,* and *leopard's band.* To insinuate that he might have made use of all of them might appear a bit extravagant, for that would give him at least the expertise of a Borgia. But that is not so ungermane for a tragedy with an Italian setting, anti-Italian sentiment being rife then in England.

To what extent could these herbs, or lack of such, have vitally affected the tragic consequences? Thematically, as I have already intimated, the allusions to rosemary may be the most suggestive; used as an emblem of both merriment and mourning, it pointed not only at marital happiness, but more significantly at the pre-Baroque, love-in-death relationship. In Gottfried Keller's adaptation of the Shakespearean tragedy, *Romeo und Julia auf dem Dorfe* (*A Village Romeo and Juliet*), the Swiss lovers engage in their nuptials while floating down the river on a bale of hay, so that when the hay sinks, they drown; it is somewhat tempting to imagine the hay as consisting of varied herbal, hemlockian properties, at least on the surrealistic level.

In any case, the friar wants the rosemary which was to have been used at Juliet's wedding to be placed on her dead body. Metaphorically, her wedding sheets thereby turn into winding sheets. Because the play as a whole has frequently been glossed as a study in "opposites"—not merely love and death, but love and hate, light and darkness, and similar oxymoronic features—the dual use given rosemary is of special symbolic import. In like manner, *parsley* was often thought of as relating wedlock to deadlock, and reverberations of this theme appear throughout the play as if aiding and abetting the herbalism (e.g., 1.5.138, 3.2.137, 5.1.34).

Because the friar presumably has some astrological interests as well as herbal ones (St. Thomas Aquinas having allowed for a certain influence of the stars), indeed even as this tragedy, as the Prologue reminds us, concerns "star-crossed lovers," the reaction of rosemary to the firmament is also *à propos.* Consider the following:

> Culpepper, the old astrological physician, in his *Complete Herbal* ... gives a long list of uses to which [rosemary] was formerly put. He begins by saying that "the sun claims privilege in it, and it is under the Celestial Ram. It is an herb of as great a use in these days as any whatsoever."[26]

Chapter II: Rosemary in Romeo and Juliet and Other Herbs

Shakespeare probably knew of such herb culture because of its extensive tradition, early treatises on it appearing as far back as the Old English *Herbarium,* which dealt with one hundred and eighty-five plants, being a translation of the writings of Apuleius, themselves based on Dioscorides' *Materia Medica.* Another work of Anglo-Saxon vintage was Cockayne's *Læceboc.* But regardless of his scholarly acquaintance with herbs, it is most probable that Shakespeare knew of Gerard's *Herbal,* which was the best known of the three major works on herbs during the Renaissance period. So it is usually cited in studies of herbal cruxes in the plays, for example in the recent interplay between Wentersdorf and Otten.[27] As the latter points out, "three major herbalists of this period are Henry Lyte, *A niewe herball, or historie of plantes* (London, 1578), which is a translation of the French version of the Cruÿdeboeck of Rembert Dodoens (Antwerp, 1554); John Gerard, *The Herball or Generall Historie of Plantes* (London, 1597), enlarged and amended by Thomas Johnson, 1633, 1636 ...; and John Parkinson, *Theatrum botanicum* (London, 1640)."[28] Some herbs had gross names, which then could have figured symbolically in the plays. Another herbal controversy worth citing is that between the authors of a study of Juliet's nurse, Liane Ferguson and Paul Yachnin, and A. Jonathan Bate.[29] The key question was whether the word *Angelica* was a reference to a culinary herb or to the name of the Nurse. The conclusion reached was that "Angelica would be an appropriate name for Lady Capulet or, with irony, the Nurse. Which of them it is must remain in doubt, but it is first and foremost a name, only secondarily a pun on the herb."[30] The First Quarto text comfortingly contains the stage direction *"Enter Nurse with hearbs...."*

The main purport of this essay is to show how herbs influenced the drama thematically; to exhibit the validity of such an enterprise we might consider first some analogies. To begin, the very concept of a garden entails a sense of structure, one which could then work its way "organically" into the dramatic form. A recent study of Renaissance gardening found formal arrangements of this kind "tangible representations of Renaissance man's conquest of the physical universe by harnessing the magical powers of nature."[31] Generally speaking, popular interest has centered on flowers, for instance in relation to *The Winter's Tale.*[32] Floral emphasis has been generated by the gardens particularly in Stratford-upon-Avon, by whether Shakespeare's title to fame might be at all understood in terms of his knowledge of country life, as evidenced in the imagery patterning detailed in Carolyn Spurgeon's well-known book or by such a study as C. Roach Smith's *The Rural Life of Shakespeare, as Illustrated by His Works*.[33] Psychological critics have shown how familiar characters like King Lear and Ophelia make garlands out of their anxieties, Lear's displaying definite herbal and medicinal properties.[34] Concern with this approach has led to such a monograph on the symbolic properties of a formal garden as Adrian Montrose's *"Curious-Knotted Garden": The Form, Themes, and Contexts of Shakespeare's "Love's Labour's Lost."*[35] Others have seen his garden scenes as mirrors held up to his characters' souls.[36] A recent study captures the metaphorical meaning of Shakespeare's rose culture.[37]

Among the more intriguing imagery studies have been ones relating herbs specifically to the outcome of tragedies. Such a paper has recently linked the mention of balm to the plight of Othello.[38] In counterpoint, a note on "Ophelia's Herbal"[39] finds her enumeration "shocking"—for reasons of prurience unnecessary to itemize here. An essay on *Romeo and Juliet* claims that the Nurse's famous digression, which includes her previously considered mention of wormwood, foreshadows a major theme of the tragedy: growth through adversity.[40] In other plays[41] the ritualistic effect of herbs and flowers lends credence to the import of these plants to the tragic structure, whereby ritualistic interest in floriculture aids and abets that in the most ritualistic genre of drama. Ritual fosters ritual. In another sense, you are what you eat, as we shall now see.

Part of the moral message of the star-crossed tragedy is that inexperience, perforce even that with herbs, can precipitate dire calamity. Proper herbalism, on the other hand, would have led to a happier dénouement. For example, even Romeo's tantrum with Tybalt could have been abated, the rash act of rushing headlong into marriage could have been tempered through herbal assistance, and in general tragic melancholia could have been clinically averted. Even if such an "herbal connection" had not been in the forefront of Shakespeare's imagination, at the same time he would scarcely have been averse to our allowing such thoughts to temper our comprehension of his stories. Thus, even as Lawson, in *The Country Housewife's Garden*, "adviseth the mistress either to be present herself or to teach her maids to know herbs from weeds,"[42] so the herbalist-critic might well be alerted to salutary plants in the plays as distinguished from mere "balefull Weedes." For even as bliss accrues

Chapter II: Rosemary in Romeo and Juliet *and Other Herbs*

from successful gardening method, so the cultivated critic can be more comfortable with proper herbal sophistication. As with Sir Hugh Plat's garden manual entitled *The Garden of Eden* (1608), "undoubtedly the favorite garden book of the early seventeenth century, particularly of the owners of the spacious gardens, was John Parkinson's *Paradisi in sole, paradisus terrestris.*"[43]

Let us consider more closely how "physick herbs" might have alleviated the Veronese tragedy. Re-enter holy thistle. If a culinary herb like this, or rue or sweet woodruff, had been successfully administered in treating victims of the plague, then Friar John presumably might not have been withheld from delivering his urgent message to Romeo, whereupon the tragic deaths would have been averted. Indeed, the following prescription is offered in *The Good Housewife's Jewell* (1585) as "A Preventive Against the Plague": "A handful each of rue, sage, sweet-briar, and elder. Bruise and strain with a quart of white wine, and put thereto a little ginger and a spoonful of the best treacle, and drink thereof morning and evening."[44] Sweet woodruff Parkinson found especially "good versus the plague."[45] Such remedies of course hinge also on the question of the basic determinism in the tragedy, on whether the astrological influences (tied, incidentally, as we have seen, to herbalism, too, in their occult way) could have been reversed. No attempt is offered to vie with Aristotle as an authority on the nature of tragedy, yet it can be doubted whether Shakespeare had read Aristotle, and besides the nature of Nature has its relevance as well, so to speak.

To come full circle and end where we began with our titular plantlife, let us simply confess that a "rose" by yet another name can metaphorically be, among other candidates of course, a simple itself. In this case rosemary becomes a leading contender. Or, to put it yet another way, as Samuel Taylor Coleridge once had it,[46] Shakespeare is himself the most singular plant in the garden of literature. In any event, the rose metaphor from the beginning was meant to accommodate rather more than the queen of flowers herself, and so this apologia is meant to pave the way for further cultivation to follow.

Notes

1. *Shakespeare's Wild Flowers: Fairy Lore, Gardens, Herbs, Gatherers of Simples and Bee Lore* (London: The Medici Society, 1935), p. 163.

2. William O. Scott, "Seasons and Flowers in *The Winter's Tale*," *Shakespeare Quarterly*, 14 (1963), 411–17, is a representative study. As for flowers that Shakespeare himself may have planted, according to Helen Noyes Webster, in *Herbs: How to Grow Them and How to Use Them* (Boston: Hale, Cushman and Flint, 1939), a treatise by Didymus Mountain (*nom de plume* of Thomas Hill) called *The Gardener's Labyrinth* may be the single most important herbal in this respect in that "it is suggested that this might have been the textbook from which Shakespeare made his own knot garden at Stratford" (p. 41). Also see the appended bibliography.

3. Annie Burnham Carter, *Shakespeare Gardens: Design, Plants, and Flower Lore* (Philadelphia: Dorrance, 1937), p. 50.

4. Anonymously and privately published (London, 1600).

5. London: Quaritch, 1896.

6. London: Thames and Hudson, 1966.

7. Folger Booklet on Tudor and Stuart Civilization (Ithaca: Cornell University Press, 1963).

8. London: E. J. Burrow, 1923.

9. Atlantic Highlands: Humanities Press, 1978.

10. London: J. G. for Nath. Brook, 1656; rpt. St. Catherine's: Provoker Press, 1968. He deals with roses too.

11. With regard to Shakespeare in particular, consider the following: Leopold Hartley Grindon, *The Shakspere Flora: A Guide to All the Principal Passages in Which Mention is Made of Trees, Plants, Flowers, and Vegetable Productions with Comments and Botanical Particulars* (Manchester: Palmer and Howe, 1883); Henry N. Ellacombe, *The Plant-Lore & Garden-Craft of Shakespeare*, 2nd ed. (London: W. Satchell, 1884); Leonard Holmesworthe, *Shakespeare's Garden: With Reference to Over a Hundred Plants* (Leamington Spa: F. Glover, 1903); James Harvey Bloom, *Shakespeare's Garden* (London: Methuen, 1903); W. Foxton, *Shakespeare Garden and Wayside Flowers: With Appropriate Quotations for Every Flower* (London: n.p., 1914); more recently, Levi Fox, *An Illustrated Introduction to "Shakespeare's*

Flowers" (Norwich, Eng.: Jarrold Colour Pubs., 1977). See also n. 9 above.

12. London: Michael Joseph, 1964, pp. 39–55.

13. Rohde, p. 167.

14. Savage, p. 244. He comments on healing herbs cited in the herbarium of the informarians.

15. Holmesworthe, p. 34.

16. Holmesworthe, p. 33.

17. Savage, p. 256.

18. The ascription is William Turner's in *Names of Herbs, in Greke Latin, Englishe, Dutche, and Frenche* (1548); see the Appendix.

19. Rohde, p. 165.

20. Rohde, loc. cit.

21. See the Appendix. Some of the items have been culled from Watt's *Bibliotheca Britannica*. The earliest original treatise on gardening extant in English was Mayster J. Gardener's *The Feate of Gardening* (1440), but since this was available in manuscript form only it is rather doubtful that Shakespeare had access to it.

22. See Christopher Devlin, *Hamlet's Divinity* (Carbondale: Southern Illinois University Press, 1963), p. 45.

23. See Bloom, p. 43.

24. Bloom, loc. cit.

25. Rohde, p. 180.

26. Savage, p. 257.

27. Karl P. Wentersdorf, "*Hamlet*: Ophelia's Long Purples," *Shakespeare Quarterly*, 29 (1978), 413–17; Charlotte F. Otten, "Ophelia's 'Long Purples' or 'Dead Men's Fingers,'" ibid., 30 (1979), 397–402.

28. Otten, pp. 397–98.

29. Liane Ferguson and Paul Yachnin, "The Name of Juliet's Nurse" (Angelica), *Shakespeare Quarterly*, 32 (1981), 95–96; A. Jonathan Bate, "An Herb By Any Other Name: *Romeo and Juliet*, IV.iv.5–6," *Shakespeare Quarterly*, 33 (1982), 336.

30. Bate, p. 336.

31. Roy Strong, *The Renaissance Garden in England* (London: Thames and Hudson, 1979).

32. See, e.g., Stanton J. Linden, "Perdita and the Gillyvors: *The Winter's Tale*, IV.iv.79–103," *Notes and Queries*, n.s. 26 (1979), 140.

33. Norwood, Pa.: Norwood Editions, 1975.

34. See, e.g., Frank McCombie, "Garlands in *Hamlet* and *King Lear*," *Notes and Queries*, n.s. 28 (1981), 132–34.

35. Salzburg: University of Salzburg Press, 1977.

36. See, e.g., Kimiko Hotta, "The Garden Imagery in Shakespeare's *Hamlet*," *Sophia Shakespeare Studies* (Jochi University, Japan), 1 (1976), 1-4.

37. Robert Rogers, *Metaphor: A Psychoanalytic View* (Berkeley: University of California Press, 1978), passim. Cf. John Vyvyan, *Shakespeare and the Rose of Love* (London: Chatto and Windus, 1960).

38. See Joan Ozark Holmer, "Othello's Threnos: 'Arabian Trees' and 'Indian' Versus 'Judean,'" *Shakespeare Studies*, 13 (1980), 145–67. (Her argument on the textual crux I dispute elsewhere; it is not germane to this particular discussion.)

39. Lucile F. Newman, "Ophelia's Herbal," *Economic Botany*, 33 (1979), 227–32.

40. William B. Toole, "The Nurse's 'Vast Irrelevance': Thematic Foreshadowings in *Romeo and Juliet*," *South Atlantic Bulletin*, 45 (1980), 21–30.

41. See, e.g., Anca Vlasopolos, "The Ritual of Midsummer: A Pattern of *A Midsummer Night's Dream*," *Renaissance Quarterly*, 31 (1978), 21–29.

42. See Eyler, p. 8.

43. Eyler, p. 11.

44. See Elinour Sinclair Rohde, *A Garden of Herbs: Being a Practical Handbook to the Making of an Old English Herb Garden* (London: The Medici Society, 1920), p. 112.

45. See Helen Morgenthau Fox, *Gardening with Herbs for Flavor and Fragrance* (New York: Macmillan, 1933), p. 109.

46. See Robert DeMaria, Jr., "Coleridgean Names," *JEGP*, 77 (1978), 343–55.

Appendix
A Selective Renaissance Bibliography of Books Relating to Herbs

Richard Banckes, *Vertues and Properties of Herbes* (1526).

Peter Treveris, *The Grete Herball* (1529).

Sir Anthony Fitz-Herbert, *The Book of Husbandry, Very Profitable and Necessary for All Persons* (1532).

William Turner, *Names of Herbs, in Greke, Latin, Englishe, Dutche, and Frenche: With the Commune Names that Herbaries and Apothecaries Use* (1548).

———, *New Herball, Book I* (1551).

———, *New Herball, Book II* (1562).

Thomas Tusser, *Five Hundred Points of Good Husbandry* (1557).

Didymus Mountain, *The Gardener's Labyrinth ... Wherein Are Set Forth, Divers Herbes* (1557).

———, *The Second Part of the Gardener's Labyrinth ... the Moste Kitchen Hearbes: With the Wittie Ordering of Other Daintie Hearbes* (1577).

Dodoens, trans. Henry Lyte, *A Newe Herbal* (1578).

William Langham, *Garden of Health* (1579).

Thomas Hylle, *A Briefe Treatyse of Gardeninge ... To Which Is Added Much Necessarie Matter, and a Number of Secretes, With the Physicke Helps Belonging to Eche Herbe* (1586).

L. Lemnius, *An Herbal for the Bible* (1587).

John Gerarde, *The Herbal; or, General History of Plants* (1597).

John Parkinson, *Paradisi in Sole, Paradisus Terrestris* (1629).

Thomas Johnson, *The Herbal; or, General History of Plants, Gathered by John Gerarde, Enlarged and Amended* (1633).

John Parkinson, *Theatrum Botanicum* (1640).

Part II

Romanticism and Roses

"lovely is the rose"
—Wordsworth

"heaven in a wild flower"
—Blake

"Tennyson and Browning are poets, and they think; but they do not feel their thoughts as immediately as the odour of a rose"
—T. S. Eliot

In this section let us cultivate some of the rose imagery found in the Sherlockian canon of Sir Arthur Conan Doyle before (more sedately) reverting to other aspects of English rose symbolism metaphorically in well-known nineteenth-century *belles lettres*. Initially, so far as the supersleuth Holmes is concerned, the link with Collins's Sergeant Cuff is clearly well worth contemplating (albeit the tempting, passing pun on "cuff link" really has to be resisted); it supplies one of the major historical sources of materials for his adventures. Although, granted, it is commonplace to compare (and, perhaps even more, contrast) the Sergeant's aesthetic retirement to love and tend roses with Holmes's own retirement to tend bees—a correlation already duly observed by Dorothy Sayers and others— surely the main connection of note is the earlier rosarian one in "The Adventure of the Naval Treaty." By and large, admittedly, it may at first seem fairly bizarre to link a private, objective-minded, misogynistic, consulting detective with Romantic or sentimentalized love of this flower, such adoration being so often more "normally" associated with aesthetes or the nature of woman. It does finally something more than merely humanize him—the way his indulgence in cocaine has been thought to.[1] It may even spiritualize him a bit, the flower at times having been thought to have just that propensity. Lest we imagine that the rose effect as accommodated to hardened detective lore is rather anomalous because of only this major link-up, let us also recall that Nero Wolfe, sometimes considered tongue-in-cheek to be Holmes's illegitimate son, had such a zest for orchids that he was popularly dubbed no less than "the largest and most famous orchid enthusiast of all."[2] Finally, Umberto Eco's recent, internationally known, bestselling novel is yet another mystery story deliberately set in the Sherlockian, or rather more aptly, Watsonian, tradition; its very title, *The Name of the Rose*, hints, as I shall show, at a borrowing from Conan Doyle. True, in his *Postscript*, Eco claimed that he fastened on this title largely because of the vagueness of rose symbolism, but the book itself points to his having made special use of Holmes on roses.[3] The novel deals, aptly enough, as its rose-window-like name implies, with monastic life, thereby complementing this book's own title and the section on roses and religion.

From Conan Doyle it is but one natural step to Charles Dickens and a symbolic rose of his, that in his last, mysteriously fragmented novel: Rosa Bud in *The Mystery of Edwin Drood*. Yet we focus not merely on the Dickens novel, rather on what has been obliquely made of it during modern times in a film, one ranked at the top in most surveys, the Welles and Mankiewicz collaboration, *Citizen Kane*. The point is that running metaphorically throughout is the key word *Rosebud*, and although admittedly too much attention can be paid to this shibboleth alone rather than to the story of human frustration it is meant to evoke,[4] we still can become validly intrigued with the inherent signification of the verbal artifice. Was it, for instance, simply a common trade name on a sled, as so many laymen still surmise? (If so, the Smithsonian Museum, which has recently inherited the last of Welles's Rosebud sleds for the film, as Welles authority Robert L. Carringer recently alerted me, has acquired substantial booty.) Or did the *Rosebud* shibboleth have rather more important, even literary bases?

One way of looking at the genesis is in seeing that Welles was originally a magician in vaudeville and so (along with Mankiewicz's help) could later have appropriated the "sled *biz*" as a cunning conjuror's mode of misdirection, but one having literary resonance as well. As a reviewer of recent studies of Welles has succinctly summed it up, "Welles, half con man, half genius, has tried—as though life were one of his magic acts—to pull the rabbit of art out of the tattered hat of improvisation."[5] The analogy is a valuable one. The reviewer went on to say succinctly that at the end of the film "when the sled is burned, the audience (but not the questing reporter) learns what 'Rosebud' means, but no man's life can be summed up in his dying words."[6] True enough, but then surely the composite meaning of "Rosebud" cannot so easily be summed up in the mere trade name of a sled either, as we shall see.

Some years ago now I first raised this issue in a brief comment in *American Notes and Queries*, and it received not only one or two Replies, but a veritable slough, one respondent even voicing the opinion that the patient editor might well assemble more Replies to this Query than to any other. The Query itself had to do with whether the key word could not have been tied in with Coleridge in

Part II: Romanticism and Roses

some fashion, for much is made in the film of his "Kubla Khan," especially his dream-induced pleasure palace called Xanadu; indirectly I suggested an ironic link with Herrick's "Gather ye rosebuds while ye may," though Ronsard could just as easily have been enlisted too, not to mention Rilke.[7]

The Replies were extraordinary. One amenable respondent then even sought out a possibly relevant reference to a rose in another Coleridge poem.[8] As if in contrast, another writer suggested that the word conveyed pure absurdity, noting that when the film was first shown during his college years, students afterwards would call out "Rosebud" when they wanted a synonym for nonsense. One helpful later reader informed me *sub rosa* (if a bit dogmatically) that the true genesis had already been well worked out in a Syracuse University dissertation, one which I had to confess I had regrettably bypassed.[9] The hopeful doctoral candidate had urged there that the most cogent source actually was not English, although he mentioned Dickens's Rosa Bud in passing, but American; it was, he thought, a resonance of Hamlin Garland's *Rose of Dutcher's Coolly* (1895). Could be.

Now having considered this tantalizing survey of possibilities invoked by Dr. Gambill's thesis, I would still respectfully beg to differ with him. For it so happens that the main connection he cites is with the same surname that is given to only a minor figure in both works: namely Thatcher. Dr. Gambill readily conceded that the parallel involves actually the inversions of sex and Thatcher as friend instead of foe (78). Moreover, when he cited Rosa Bud, he did so simply as only in a single, factually misleading sentence, claiming that she was an orphan who did not have a happy marriage (77). In point of fact, however, she never wed Edwin nor anyone else in the completed part of the projected novel, a marriage having been *arranged* for her only. Plausibly Dr. Gambill had his own ideas, as indeed have so many, regarding how the mystery would have ended, but, in any event, he paid it, in its present form, remarkably short shrift.

The Replies received to the "Rosebud" note I then composed were fairly enlightening. Some cautious readers evidently saw the tell-tale Dickensian effect as underscoring the Freudian interpretation. Some recent critics, moreover, notably Everett Bleiler,[10] a well-known authority on mysteries, have discerned some promiscuous resonances in the little sobriquet Edwin bestowed on her: namely Pussy. That suspicion would tie in with the ingenious

Welles-Mankiewicz usage in that the former apparently chose to downgrade the Rosebud artifice as "a rather cheap Freudian gimmick," thereby merely "dollar book Freud." But the main Freudian allusion would seem to be to Kane's childhood relation to his mother, not to sexuality in general. Even so Welles later had his bed made into the form of a gigantic Rosebud sled. In any case, I strongly doubt whether Dickens himself would originally have wanted any special *risqué* effect, even as Rosa's literal pet name has had sedate enough meaning even to this day in England. Thus "*Puss(e)y* comes from *Pewsey* or *Pusey* which are parishes in Wiltshire and Berkshire" and "once referred to a girl."[11] The contemporary, successful English play *The Dresser* has a Pussy, the name of the girl playing Cordelia. Because of the obvious pet association with *pussycat*, the nickname of *Kitty* is surely comparable. Stanley Kaufmann, in his review of André Bazin's *Orson Welles*, cited François Truffaut's preface as critical of Welles's own criticism of the Rosebud device, terming *Kane* "the best serious American film."[12]

Probably the prize response to the view that "Rosebud" conveys Freudian innuendoes is that provided by Kaufmann: "The only Freudian falsity in the Rosebud idea that I can see is its abstraction from a complex of other psychological elements, but the script makes the abstraction quite clear—no one clue can explain a human being—and in any event it is not used as a Freudian explanation but as a (memorably effective) dramaturgical device."[13] Comparable is Truffaut's criticism: "I must confess that I don't share [Welles's] viewpoint: Rosebud seems to be as good as Ali Baba's 'Open Sesame'. . . ."[14] Such viewpoints are eminently fair, but it should go without saying that the question of whether or not the artifice was *consciously* utilized as a Freudian device is beside the point, Freud obviously having concerned himself with the *un*conscious. Further, the rosebud/sexuality association may derive finally from the familiar flower or figleaf covering genital areas in traditional paintings. As is commonly known, the closeness of the rose to love is the subject of *Le Roman de la Rose.*

In general, the cardinal meaning of "Rosebud" was that derived from Dickens. After all, the common nickname *Puss* is so frequently taken to refer to a young girl that Edwin's use of the diminutive *Pussy* sounds *au courant* enough without sexual *double entendre*. Hence to invest a pet name with gross connotations is to be more modern—than Victorian. In any event, Welles and Mankiewicz based

Part II: Romanticism and Roses

their film largely on the life of William Randolph Hearst, whose own manifest Dickensian predilections and his calling his own childhood sweetheart by the very same pet name, as I shall show, indubitably enter in.

In concluding this section with reference to the poppy as well (and hence drug use), I base myself on that flower as (alas) the metaphoric Rose of Love. The influence of drugs on literature of the time can hardly be underestimated, however distasteful some uses of it may appear. Even the conscientious Holmes was at one sad time a cocaine *habitué* (or at least until his faithful *confrère*, Dr. Watson, "weaned" him from the addiction); John Jasper, in *Edwin Drood*, a formally respected choirmaster but still the main suspect, was analogously an opium addict. Hence in my investigation of the drug scene, I have felt compelled to focus somewhat on S. T. Coleridge, whose most familiar poetic inspiration in "Kubla Khan" he recorded at least as opium-induced. True, some skeptics have urged that he simply made up the account of how the poem came to him, that he purposely embellished the Romantic effect and never had the reverie-dream which produced the lyric supposedly that he afterwards wrote down. Yet Wordsworth, who presumably should have known, if anyone, later claimed that his friend did really believe he had had that dream. For, in reporting a conversation with the Laureate Wordsworth, on 19 December 1830, Henry Alford stated that "certainly Coleridge believes" the poem "was actually composed in a dream."[15]

In any event, I have delved somewhat into the sociological and medical aspects of this drug issue *en passant*, partly as a result of being Book Review Editor of *Journal of Human Relations* with access to current books on the subject. Both Lewis Carroll's Alice and L. Frank Baum's Land of Oz entered the fantastic picture.[16] In concentrating on "Kubla Khan," I have attempted to try to come to terms with its universality, which T. S. Eliot once questioned by claiming its imagery had not truly been "*used*," as he put it; indeed, Coleridge himself had first described it as little else than "a psychological curiosity." The exotic subject led me to an avocation: to try to see in just how many journals around the world I might place essays on this little masterpiece; I succeeded in Canada, England, the Netherlands, Japan, and India (thrice). Perhaps these will some day be assembled, but in the present collection only two items are relevant, because of their connection with the "Rose of Love."

The first essay discusses the influence of the poppy in terms of the last stanza considered as a kind of apologia. In other words, after Coleridge was interrupted in writing down his pipe-dream by the celebrated intruder from Porlock, he apparently felt obliged to confirm his inability to accomplish the original task in the mode he had wanted. So he chose a concluding stanza to tell the story as a kind of moral or coda. Such a dry explanation may not appear, at first, very "Romantic." It would also presuppose that, for better or for worse, he was not guilty of perpetrating a hoax in his published description of the poem's genesis. In any case, my essay pertains to the addictive effect of the opium drug as it later affected Coleridge in his poem "The Pains of Sleep." Because the precursor of my paper appeared in an out-of-the-way pedagogical journal, its lack of ready access justifies its inclusion here. Neither this chapter nor my working draft for the next, for example, are included in Frank Jordan and M. Schulz's standard review of research and criticism on the English Romantics, albeit Schulz does happen to cite five other articles of mine on the poem (two in an introductory paragraph). He appears to be biassed against source-study as outmoded, a curious enough verdict when this poem and Lowes's *The Road to Xanadu* are borne in mind, though the latter's seminal study and its aftermath may make some readers feel saturated with such an approach. Hence when I tried to consider one Xanaduvian venture of mine as a non-source-study, but rather a jeu d'esprit, he contended that its interest is really otherwise and that it has only "a touch of jeu d'esprit."[17]

My second essay relating to "Kubla Khan," namely "'Pot Luck,'" has already been briefly discussed. As formerly a review-article, it deals with books treating the subject from the abstract to the concrete, the first originally being on drugs in general, the last on the poem itself.[18] The last essay represents my latest endeavor; in marked contrast to Lowes, it deals with a road *from* rather than *to* Xanadu. Although accepted several years ago by *Research Studies* (Washington State University), it was not printed because the journal folded. I would attempt to justify its inclusion because its ideas received the gracious approbation of Thomas McFarland, as I point out at the end.

Part II: Romanticism and Roses

How finally does "Kubla Khan" relate to the glamorous subject of roses? First, my main title invites "a rose by another name," in this case metaphorically with the opium as the Rose of Love (however questionable that designation); secondly, my subtitle allows for the poppy, too, as yet another specifically floricultural focus; and, thirdly, let us bear in mind that whereas the opium poppy can lead to ill effects, it is thereby not so far removed from its more domestic cousin, the rose, which in its own way amorously is known for producing at least a fever.

Notes

1. I owe this point to Jack Tracy's keynote address at our first area Sherlockian conference in 1981 at Central State University, Ohio. As for the old prejudice that roses attract women more than men, it is common knowledge that rose societies attract more males, probably because most rosarians are male horticulturalists.

2. Correspondence in the *Smithsonian,* January 1986, pp. 18—in response to an article on the orchid.

3. See R. F. Fleissner, "A Rose Based on a Rose Based on a Rose: From Collins to Doyle to Eco," presented at the conference "Roses and the Arts" (see Ch. XV); published in revised form as "The Master Sleuth Accommodated," *The Sherlock Holmes Review,* 2,1 (1988), 15–20, 42.

4. See Robert L. Carringer, "Rosebud, Dead or Alive: Narrative and Symbolic Structure in *Citizen Kane,*" *PMLA,* 91 (1976), 185–93. This article, only one of a number of his works on this subject, has lent due academic status to a masterwork previously given short shrift. I am grateful to him for providing me with some valuable pointers in personal correspondence.

5. Gerald Weales on Barbara Leaming's *Orson Welles* (1985) and Charles Higham's *Orson Welles: The Rise and Fall of an American Genius* (1985) in the *Smithsonian,* January 1986, p. 156.

6. Weales, p. 157.

7. E.g., see the headnote to Part III. For the Ronsard connection, I am indebted to Pierre L. Horn. Cf. his "Cueillez dès aujourd'hui les roses de la vie" (from "A Hélène").

8. Hartmut Breitkreuz, "Rosebud," *American Notes and Queries*, 11, 1 (Sept., 1972), 10, notes that Brit. Mus. Add. MS. 27, 902 provides an STC variant of note: "Rose-bud."

9. Norman Paul Gambill, "*Citizen Kane*: An Art Historical Analysis," diss. Syracuse, 1976. I have, since then, investigated and found it serviceable, if scarcely definitive.

10. "The Names in *Drood*, Part I," *Dickens Quarterly*, 1 (1984), 88–93.

11. Robert M. Rennick, "Obscene Names and Naming in Folk Tradition," in *Names and Their Varieties: A Collection of Essays in Onomastics*, compiled by Kelsie B. Harder (Lanham, Maryland: University Press of America in cooperation with the American Name Society, 1986), p. 170.

12. *TLS*, 10 Nov. 1978, p. 1308.

13. Kaufmann, p. 1306.

14. Kaufmann, loc. cit.

15. See the *Life of Henry Alford* (1871), p. 62—as cited by F. W. Bateson, *The Scholar-Critic* (London: Routledge and Kegan Paul, 1972), p. 56.

16. See R. F. Fleissner, "Drugs: A Pressing Problem (With Side Comments on Oz & Alice)," *Journal of Human Relations* (Central State University, Ohio), 20 (1972), 499–502.

17. *The English Romantic Poets: A Review of Research and Criticism*, 4th ed., ed. Frank Jordan, M. Schulz, et al. (New York: The Modern Lang. Assn., 1985), p. 380.

18. The first of these, Herman W. Land's *What You Can Do About Drugs and Your Child* (New York: Hart Publ. Co., 1969), may be a bit dated now and so is not considered here. Also relevant would be *A Preventive Approach to Drug Abuse Education: Proceedings of the 1970 Central State University Summer Workshop on Prevention of Drug Abuse*, ed. S. Louise Garcia and Michael Quigley (Privately printed, 1970).

Chapter III

A Rose by Another Name: The Floral Digression in *The Naval Treaty*— Regrafted

During the Vietnam War years a paper printed in the ever provocative journal of The Baker Street Irregulars ventured the timely thesis that Sherlock Holmes presents himself as, of all things, the original "hippie." That anachronism notwithstanding, the first piece of evidence given is worth reconsidering:

> It is very fashionable, in the hippie movement today, to love flowers. This is not a new romance, gentlemen, on the contrary. In *The Naval Treaty*, you will recall, Holmes said, "What a lovely thing a rose is! ... Our highest assurance of the goodness of Providence seems to me to rest in the flowers."[1]

The essay was then adorned with a comical sketch of the Conan Doyle supersleuth primly sniffing, in a quaintly introspective manner, a majestic rose with Dr. Watson looking on apprehensively. For if Holmes was supposed to have been concentrating his faculties on locating a purloined treaty in Dupin-like fashion for the stalwart British navy, why then was he letting his keen mind wander?

The premise of the present essay is that the world's first consulting detective, if that label still applies, was really not the first but the second "hippie" (though we would scarcely want now to update that to say also "yuppie") insofar as his action was prominently preëmpted by Sergeant Cuff in Wilkie Collins's classic sovereign mystery, *The Moonstone*. The value of such a correlation is that it could make Conan Doyle's master sleuth seem at least less idiosyncratic in his indulgence if he had a recognizable, model precedent; a forerunner would at least be more comfortable to those accepting the modern penchant for behavioral norms.

Hence, one use of a sleuth's floral *mis*direction, Collins's, that is, may paradoxically redirect us to another such effect, Conan Doyle's. Because the leading monograph treating thoroughly the Collins-Doyle literary relation is rather difficult to come by nowadays,[2] the present essay justifies itself. Other glosses of late on the novel have been studiously avoiding the clear-cut Collinsian correlations. Dorothy L. Sayers, for example, jumped from rose gardening to mere pollination by sensing something less than a roseate link between Holmes and Cuff: "One can believe that [Cuff] made a success of his rose-growing when he retired; he genuinely loved roses, whereas one can never feel that the great Sherlock possessed quite the right feeling for his bees."[3] (Doubtless she was ignorant of the import of *A Taste of Honey*, now recognized as one of the best of the pastiches.) Moreover, William Baring-Gould's limited gloss on the digression in *The Naval Treaty* reads as follows: "This is the only passage in the long Saga in which Holmes speaks forthrightly of religion. Compare *Matt.* 6: 'Consider the lilies of the field. . . .'"[4] Such an oblique gloss to the Sermon on the Mount is hardly "religion" in any formal sense, though.

Although we would not want our present essay to detract from any valid biblical gloss (if some soul may be saved thereby), let us consider some relevant Sherlockian minutiae now in the two curiously analogous episodes in the stories, technically studies in digression and misdirection. In the story of the stolen treaty, the bland, blasé detective, without a moment's warning, shifts his line of interest from the theft to a panegyric on the pulchritude of the rose, both physically and symbolically. In a split second, he justifies his abrupt aesthetic turn by finding the queen of flowers to be stark evidence of the Deity's marked love of His Creation and inferring that such faith is not outside the ken of the ardent detector of crime if only because "there is nothing in which deduction is so necessary as in religion." (By implication, we revert to the familiar Anselmian syllogism on the proof for God's existence. Yet, ironically enough, the formally logical approach to religion may also be seen as its limitation, even as theism depends so little on actual factual data or inductive method.) Holmes thus goes into a "reverie," which, in point of fact, lasts "some minutes" with the rose poised primly and securely between his lanky fingers. Then he is interrupted, in his apparent absentmindedness, by curtly being reminded about the practical naval mystery to be solved. (At this point context indicates that rose adoration is not itself a form of mystery so much as a mystique, indulgence in a bit of Romantic pantheism.)

In counterpoint, in the twelfth chapter of *The Moonstone*, also fairly promptly in the narrative, the celebrated Sergeant Cuff arrives on the scene, whereupon the first maneuver he makes is to proceed straight to the rosebed. As Julian Symons tells us, "Cuff is the first master of the apparently irrelevant report, the unexpected observation. Faced with a difficult problem and asked what is to be done, he trims his nails with a penknife and suggests a turn in the garden and a look at the roses...."[5] The butler-narrator, not unlike the subservient Watson, experiences disapprobation, is astonished at such seemingly insouciant sentimentality. Cuff's discursus on the rose is rather longer than Holmes's, and is carried on at intervals later, for clearly he venerates it in a similar, but even more intense manner. In both cases, as it happens, a lady becomes involved, something valuable is stolen, and some allusion is made to religious mysticism, though the Sergeant's own aesthetic justification for such a divagation is rather different from Holmes's. Still, in finding a man's personal tastes often unrelated to his profession, Cuff discerns a proper answer accounting for the surprised reactions not only in the fiction in which he appears but *The Naval Treaty*. Lest these general parallels appear to be coincidental only, some elaboration must follow.

As a starter, Cuff dwells on what he dubs several times the famed "musk-rose" (82); the species is, verbally at least, similar enough to Holmes's focus, the "moss-rose." Secondly, the nostalgic Sergeant is described "fondling the musk-rose with his lanky fingers, and speaking to it as if he was speaking to a child"; analogously, Holmes lapses into "a reverie, with the moss-rose between his fingers." Such sensitive concentration bespeaks true intimacy with one's subject. Thirdly, Collins solemnly invokes "God" in passing, whereas Holmes cites "Providence" along with "religion" more abstractly. As expected, the theological twist of these roses has raised some comment. We might meditate on it.

Entertainingly, D. Martin Dakin, for example, at first stated sharply, "His philosophical disquisition on the moss rose has aroused the fury of scientific persons, who maintain that the colour and scent of the rose are not the extras from which Holmes deduced the goodness of Providence, but necessities in that they attract insect fertilisers."[6] Dakin then fortunately combatted this dry demurrer aptly enough and upheld what he hastened to term the master sleuth's "religious sensitiveness." The next problem is whether any basis for such adoration of the unworldly was anticipated in the Collins context. Such a parallel would not have to detract from the genuineness of Holmes's own feelings, but could give them support. To resort to a commonplace caveat, "mysticism" in itself is apt to be too close to *mist* and *schism* otherwise.

Because Cuff's passing reference to the Almighty may be taken here as little more than an offhand ejaculation ("please God"), let us consider two possible anagogical clues: allusion to the rose garden as a "rosery" (thereby suggesting the added, blurred but homophonic effect of *rosary*) and, in the same context, "a circle set in a square," which recalls the eternal conundrum of squaring the circle. The latter represents a divine, geometrical miracle, one cited appropriately at the very end of Dante's *raffinierte Divina Commedia*, where the Rose symbol is strongly emphasized. Likewise it occurs in John Donne's Holy Sonnet commencing "At the *round* earth's *imagined corners*, blow your trumpets, angels. . . ." (Donne was assuredly much indebted to Dante.) Especially because these religious overtones were not original with Collins they probably meant something to Conan Doyle, if partly because of his own early Catholic upbringing and Jesuit education and owing to his strong predilection for literary allusion and medieval lore, which was duly resurrected in his historical romances and some short stories. Soon, moreover, we learn of Cuff's own spiritual fervor, as when he states, "The ugly women have a bad time of it in the world; let's hope it will be made up to them in another"—truly a gallant sense of proper Christian resignation. A moment later, he adds, "I won't take a rose. It goes to my heart to break them off the stem" (95). Just before, right after the narrator cites St. Paul's reference to the darkness of the present world—"(as the Scripture says) 'in a glass darkly'" (93)—Cuff switches again from speaking of the moonstone mystery to the rose garden.

To be fair, a contrast looms as well: whereas Cuff refers to "our old English rose holding up his head along with the best" (82), Holmes's flower dangles sadly from a "drooping stalk." That unhappy, slight discrepancy, however, would scarcely make the overall floral comparison itself wilt. Clearly Cuff's warm, affirmative explanation, "Pretty dear!" is emotionally akin to Holmes's own, "What a lovely thing a rose is!" The Sergeant's admiration of this flower is cited as becoming his "trick" (96), for he later is described as often resorting to rose culture, notably to calmly humming "The Last Rose of Summer" at odd moments, even as Holmes's mention of religion, symbolized by the same flower, is sometimes thought to be an indication of his deeper spiritual nature, which also crops up at times elsewhere, if not in a very dominant or consistent manner.

In his opening scene Cuff's "long lanky fingers" neatly point forward to Holmes holding his bloom as he would his spyglass. In the same context, Cuff's face, "as sharp as a hatchet" (81), provides a profile suggestive of Holmes's features, his hawk-like nose in particular. Finally a whiff of "the sea-air" duly cited by Collins as "very brisk and refreshing" (81) hints at Conan Doyle's *Naval Treaty* in subject-matter. Such a connection in itself may at first appear slight, but we then recall how much is made of the beach effect in Collins's novel, notably with such weird emphasis upon "the shivering sands" throughout. In short, we have a littoral parallel.

Clearly the standard anagogical symbolism associated with rose imagery down through the ages—from Dante to Constable to Blake and to so many others—suggests that Conan Doyle was hardly obligated to turn simply to Collins for his extra aesthetic "embellishment" (as Holmes terms the import of the rose), but still some likelihood is evident that he did make good use of *The Moonstone*. Likewise Collins may, in turn, have been indebted to literary giants like Shakespeare and Keats on the value of the muskrose.[7] But in the case of Doyle, he turned to Collins as forerunner in other respects: in *The Sign of the Four* and "Uncle Jeremy's Household" (a pre-Sherlockian tale)[8] he made use of the same tonal kind of Indian background as evident in *The Moonstone*. Indeed, Jack Tracy has authoritatively argued that Conan Doyle never had the Jeremy story reprinted specifically because the debt to Collins's masterpiece might have seemed too self-evident to his readers.[9] In any event, Conan Doyle's well-known appreciation of Dickens's works, which themselves were so akin to Collins's at times,[10] would point to yet another vital enough indebtedness.

In Gillettean terms, Holmes tipped his venerable deerstalker to Collins in *The Naval Treaty*.[11] In regrafting the literary roses, we see further how Conan Doyle's own floral arrangement, as it were, was thereby recrafted. Thus when Cuff retires, he too seeks the *moss*-rose, not merely the musk.[12] The "name of the rose" is, in a word, moss, as Umberto Eco might say, for he, too, took over passages from Collins and Conan Doyle in his so-called anti-detective novel.[13]

Notes

1. David A. Wallace, "Sherlock Holmes, the First Hippie," *The Baker Street Journal*, n.s. 19 (1969), 47. Wallace's paper, which was first delivered to a Sherlockian scion society, offered several other points besides the evidence of Holmes's comments prefiguring those of the so-called "flower people." As for the heretical suggestion that Holmes's inclination could seriously have revealed androgynous tendencies, we may leave that to the psychobiologists.

2. See the aforementioned study by Liljegren. T. S. Blakeney, in "*The Moonstone* (1868)—Wilkie Collins," *Sherlock Holmes Journal*, 11 (Winter 1972), 19–21, relates the novel only to *The Man with the Twisted Lip, A Study in Scarlet*, and *The Resident Patient*.

3. "The Omnibus of Crime," rpt. in *The Art of the Mystery Story: A Collection of Critical Essays*, ed. Howard Haycraft (New York: Carroll and Graf, 1983), p. 90. Did not Holmes's bees derive somehow from Cuff's roses?

4. *The Annotated Sherlock Holmes*, 2 vols. (New York: Clarkson W. Potter, 1967), II, 178. He also reproduces Sidney Paget's illustration of Holmes sniffing the rose (from the *Strand Magazine*, Oct. 1893). References to *The Moonstone* are to the Random House ed. (1937), those to Conan Doyle to *The Complete Sherlock Holmes*, introd. Christopher Morley (New York: Doubleday, 1927).

5. *The Detective Story in Britain* (London: F. Milder and Sons, 1969), p. 12. In comparison, see Rosemary Herbert, "Interview with Jeremy Brett," *The Armchair Detective*, 18 (1985), 340–50, especially her account of Brett's reporting that there is "a wonderful description ... of Holmes moving through the rose garden 'like a golden retriever'" (348).

6. *A Sherlock Holmes Commentary*, p. 136.

7. See Willard Spiegelman, "Keats's 'Coming Muskrose' and Shakespeare's 'Profound Verdure,'" *ELH*, 50 (1983), 347–62. He

sees *A Midsummer Night's Dream* as the source of the "coming muskrose" in "Ode to a Nightingale."

8. See R. F. Fleissner's study (originally read at a conference at Wright State U.) on "Uncle Jeremy's Household" as "The First Baker Street Mystery" story (hence *ur*-Sherlockian) in *Canadian Holmes* (Toronto), 12, 3 (1989), 19–25.

9. *Masterworks of Crime and Mystery by Sir Arthur Conan Doyle*, ed. Jack Tracy (New York: Dial, 1982), pp. 91–92. The debt to Dickens, particularly to *Copperfield*, was already very strong.

10. Notably in *Bleak House* and *Edwin Drood*. It also should be noted that *The Moonstone* first appeared serially in a journal that Dickens edited. Conan Doyle also published stories in Dickens's *All the Year Round*: "That Veteran" and "Gentlemanly Joe." These have now been reproduced, with an introduction, in *33 by Arthur Conan Doyle*, compiled and edited by John Michael Gibson and Richard Lancelyn Green (New York: Avenel Books, 1982).

11. T. S. Eliot, in "Wilkie Collins and Dickens" (1927), briefly associated Holmes with Cuff and rated Collins's masterwork as the greatest of mysteries. See his *Selected Essays, 1917–1932* (New York: Harcourt, Brace, 1932), p. 377. See also Trevor H. Hall's chapter on Eliot and Conan Doyle in his *Sherlock Holmes and His Creator* (London: Duckworth, 1978), pp. 45–54, especially p. 47. For another obvious debt to Cuff, consider Inspector Ruff in Patrick Hamilton's popular drama *Angel Street: A Victorian Thriller* (cinematically better known as *Gaslight*), which I directed at Spring Hill College, Mobile, Alabama (1959).

12. P. 242. In all fairness, however, the Cuff-Holmes parallel *in toto* is not altogether helpful, if only because the former fails to solve the Moonstone case. Moreover, another figure in the novel also suddenly pauses, arresting the action and chain of thought, to pick flowers and exclaim about them, namely Ezra Jennings (p. 297), who, like Holmes, takes drugs. Still, Cuff makes much also of a paint stain, and it may not be altogether coincidental that *The Naval Treaty* starts off with reference to *The Adventure of the Second Stain*. Cuff is surely as much a precursor of Holmes here as is Poe's Dupin. (Conan Doyle's debt to the latter is too well known to require special documentation.) On mysticism in general in *The Moonstone*, which might have inspired Holmes's religious fervor, see Mark M. Hennelly, Jr., "Detecting Collins' Diamond: From Serpentstone to

Moonstone," *Nineteenth Century Fiction*, 39 (June 1984), 25–47. Also concerned with symbolic meaning is Patricia Miller Frick's "Wilkie Collins's 'Little Jewel': The Meaning of *The Moonstone*," *Philological Quarterly*, 63 (1984), 313–21. As to whether Holmes's oddly referring to "seven" clues in this story has some added mystical (i.e. numerological) association, cf. Dakin, loc. cit. (albeit he refers to this number of clues as only "magical").

13. See, e.g., Stefano Tani, *The Doomed Detective: The Contribution of the Detective Novel to Postmodern American and Italian Fiction* (Carbondale: Southern Illinois University Press, 1984). For further data on Holmes and roseate imagery, see Richard Milner, "Sherlock Holmes and the Mystery of the Red Rose," *Baker Street Journal*, n.s. 37 (1987), 162–64; on detectives and flora in general, see *Murder Ink*, perpetrated by Dilys Winn (New York: Workman Pub. Co., 1977), pp. 477–79.

Chapter IV

The Germination of "Rosebud" in *Citizen Kane*: The Dickensian Bulb

Although it is commonly held that Orson Welles's talisman "Rosebud" in his most famous film, indeed perhaps *the* most famous, *Citizen Kane*, is a trade name on a sled,[1] to claim that such a manufacturing source is the only or leading one is bound to appear prosaic, underscoring the monetary *cliché* "Business is business." Nor does it help much to endorse the term as simply a Freudian artifice, "rather dollar book Freud," as Welles called it, alluding to the effect of its originator, H. Mankiewicz.[2] Along these lines, the following gloss has recently been suggested, is helpful enough, but also rather limited in its overall, final perspective:

> The name itself, Rosebud, refers to an early stage of a flower, a stage full of potential for growth.... Kane's murmuring of the word on his deathbed perhaps expresses his sense that his original potential as a human being was never realized.

Likewise:

> It is significant that Kane first utters the word "Rosebud" right after Susan has left him and that his memory of the sled is triggered by the snow scene in the glass globe which is her possession (it can be seen in her boarding house room the first time Kane meets her). Susan herself seems to be connected with Rosebud and with Kane's childhood.[3]

Welles admitted that he himself, and not Mankiewicz, composed the key line "Maybe Rosebud was something [Kane] couldn't get or something he lost."[4] Hence it is safe to say that the wily producer had some inkling of the intense symbolism behind the word, that it probably ultimately stood for the name of a girl.

With this notion in mind, we may be struck, in reading *The Mystery of Edwin Drood*, how the hero named the girl he eventually loses *Rosebud* (as a variant or abbreviated form of Rosa Bud). Further research reveals that the Dickensian allusion is the only one cited in a standard literary reference work, *The New Century Handbook of English Literature*, under the entry *Rosebud*[5] and that Welles was particularly enamored of Dickens's novels. Indeed, critics have pointed to the unique Dickensian flavor of the film. For example, Kane "rises to manhood in a series of Dickensian scenes"; there is that "vivid, thoroughly Dickensian scene" when Kane arrives at the *Inquirer* offices for the first time. Moreover, "Dickens in his humorous mood" is said to have set "the tone of all these characterizations, as well as that of the pace of the first half of the film, with its boisterous allegro clip, its procession of grotesques...."[6] It is surely no coincidence that the very next film Welles wanted to make after *Citizen Kane* was one on *Pickwick Papers*.

Further, the influence of Dickens on Welles is provocatively subtle. For instance, his film on Falstaff was originally called *Chimes at Midnight*, derived most probably from Dickens's own famous appropriation of the well-known Shakespearean line "We have heard the chimes at midnight, Master Shallow" as found in his novella *The Chimes*. In a famous production of *The Merry Wives of Windsor*, Dickens also played Shallow. Because no one in his right mind would doubt Welles's strong debt to nineteenth-century Romanticism—as evidenced especially in his emphasis on the witchcraft in his film of *Macbeth*—the Dickens connection is a natural one to make.[7]

If *The Mystery of Edwin Drood* is the raw material that germinated the Rosebud image, can it be said to have any thematic kinship besides describing a lost love? The answer is positive for several reasons. First, the most obvious literary source for *Citizen Kane* is, granted, not Dickens but Coleridge's "Kubla Khan," quoted notably at the outset. *Kane*, in a sense, represents a modernization of *Khan*. The lyric is famous, or notorious, as is well known, for having been opium-inspired, though it is sometimes argued that the vain poet

Chapter IV: The Germination of "Rosebud" in Citizen Kane

exaggerated the effects of the drug. The *Drood* novel also deals with the influence of opium and has similar references to the Far and Near East, to China and Egypt. Chinese appear in the opening chapter, and Drood wants to travel to Egypt, the land of the Nile, which happens to be one of the proposed sources for "the sacred river" in "Kubla Khan." On a subtler level, both the Coleridge poem and Dickens novel reveal a debt to the witchcraft element in *Macbeth*,[8] an overtone attractive to Welles. Finally, both "Kubla Khan" and the novel shared the common Romantic convention of being unfinished and hence open-ended. Even this correlation ties in with Citizen Kane's Xanadu, an estate which was also left uncompleted.

Yet another obvious source for Kane's Rosebud image is doubtless the most famous one in the annals of literature, Herrick's resonant line "Gather ye rosebuds while ye may," and that also was behind Dickens's use of the name, for the Romantic link in the amorous sense is obvious.

But an even more tantalizing connection emerges: Drood dared call his Rosebud "Pussy." Such a nickname may appear to be funny or gross on this side of the Atlantic but has been quite acceptable in England. Mankiewicz, in gathering *his* rosebud material from Mrs. Fremont Older's biography of William Randolph Hearst, would have noted that young William "pointed out the rose buds to Pussy,"[9] the pet name of his childhood friend Katherine Soulé. Robert Carringer first pointed out the significance of this allusion as one to Welles's Rosebud in "The Scripts of *Citizen Kane*,"[10] but he ignored entirely the Dickensian undertones and finally supplanted his finding with his emphasis upon "Rosebud" as a trademark in the manufacturing industry. The point came in for debate in open forum during a panel discussion on Welles at the 1979 Ohio Shakespeare Conference at the University of Toledo, to which I happened to be privy.

Lest we think that the rosebud/Pussy association was no more than sheer coincidence, we need note only that Mrs. Older took pains to emphasize Hearst's fondness for Dickens. (Not so surprisingly, perhaps, the financier was especially taken by *Dombey and Son*, the title already suggesting its commercial motif.) "Charles Dickens, his first literary hero," she wrote and then warmed up, "and his literary hero of all time, the one writer that has most completely satisfied Hearst." She went on the explain just how the Inimitable came to inspire the prototype for Citizen Kane: "In this novelist Will found richness and variety of humor, riotous fancy, unequaled genius for characterization, sympathy for humanity and a desire to better the conditions of the world of which he never tired"; she noted that "again and again he reads the English novelist," that "in Hearst's conversation there are frequent references to Dickens," and that, even when she was writing the biography, "the favorite writers of his own staff are those who have come under Dickens's sway."[11] And that is not all.[12] So it would appear clear enough that Mankiewicz, if not Welles himself, also came under Dickens's sway when associating the rosebud/Pussy image with both Hearst and *Drood*—a subliminal correlation.

The reporter in the film, in being asked to discover the meaning of Kane's dying shibboleth "Rosebud," is told (or given this directive): "Rosebud, dead or alive." Among the clues in the film as to the meaning of this key word are the following: "racehorse?" "It will probably turn out to be a very simple thing," his wife Emily herself being "no rosebud" (nor was Susy), "a piece of a jigsaw puzzle," and perhaps "all he really wanted out of life was love." More is implied than the standard answer: the sled—a classic case of misdirection (Welles having originally been a clever magician in vaudeville). The best answer may be hinted at in the newspaper editor's phrase "dead or alive." The analogous point is that Dickens had many alternate titles selected for *The Mystery of Edwin Drood*, but his principal one was the same: *Dead? Or Alive?* That title, in effect, spells out the mystery behind *Edwin Drood*—and of "Rosebud" in *Citizen Kane*.[13] As a final touch, curiously enough when the pet name "Rosebud" is first cited in the Dickens novel, so is the most common onomastic variant of the filmmaker: "Wells." They inhabit the same page.[14]

Notes

1. For discussion of this problem following the wake of *The Citizen Kane Book* (Boston: Little, Brown, 1971), see R. F. Fleissner, "Rosebud," in *American Notes and Queries*, 10 (1972), 103, which engendered responses in the issues of Sept. 1972 and May 1973.

2. Welles's reference to "Rosebud" as Freudian is cited by Robert L. Carringer, 188. His essay is reductive in that it minimizes the

Chapter IV: The Germination of "Rosebud" in Citizen Kane   57

import of the name as such (his title in a sense being ironic). See also n. 10 below.

3. James F. Maxwell, "'A Man Like Ourselves': *Citizen Kane* as Aristotelian Tragedy," *Literature / Film Quarterly*, 14 (1986), 200.

4. Peter Bogdanovich, "The Kane Mutiny," *Esquire*, Oct. 1972, p. 182.

5. Ed. Clarence L. Barnhart (New York: Appleton-Century-Crofts, 1956), p. 177.

6. Charles Higham, *The Films of Orson Welles* (Berkeley: University of California Press, 1970), pp. 27–28. See also M. L. Campbell's published response to me (n. 1 above) for further Dickensian overtones.

7. For more on the Dickens-Shakespeare association, see my *Dickens and Shakespeare: A Study in Histrionic Contrasts* (New York: Haskell House, 1965; rpt. 1969); also Alfred B. Harbage, *A Kind of Power: The Shakespeare-Dickens Analogy*, Jayne Lectures for 1974 (Philadelphia: American Philosophical Soc., 1975).

8. See H. Duffield, "The *Macbeth* Motif in *Edwin Drood*," *The Dickensian*, 30 (1934), 263–71; G. Wilson Knight, *The Starlit Dome* (London: Methuen, 1941), p. 245.

9. *William Randolph Hearst: American* (New York: Appleton-Century, 1936), p. 19.

10. *Critical Inquiry*, 5 (1978), 384.

11. Older, p. 40.

12. She has more on Dickens and Hearst on p. 38.

13. See Felix Aylmer, *The Drood Case* (New York: Barnes and Noble, 1964), p. 187 ("The Notes"); also R. F. Fleissner, "*Drood* the Obscure: The Evidence of the Names," *The Armchair Detective*, 13 (1980), 12–16.

14. Charles Dickens, *The Mystery of Edwin Drood* (New York: New American Library, 1967), p. 25.

Chapter V

Opium as the Rose of Love: "Kubla Khan" Revisited

It has been previously suggested that the caveat at the tail end of "Kubla Khan" might well be taken as a moral against illicit use of hard drugs. When this suggestion was first made, it met with some apparent disfavor apparently because the didactic approach seemed too pedagogical for discussing an English Romantic, who himself was so often reacting to the didacticism of the previous century, or even too unaesthetic for a discussion of literature *qua* literature. (On the other hand, it is useful again here to bear in mind that in his celebrated essay on "Hamlet and His Problems," T. S. Eliot argued that, *qua* literature, it cannot be discussed because there is simply nothing to discuss.[1]) In short, a purely aesthetic approach to the literary artifact presumably would preclude entertaining such a moral at the end. For, as Archibald MacLeish so tersely has stated it, "A poem should not mean / But be." On the other hand, MacLeish's very poetic truth represents a final moral to his *Ars Poetica* and thus is in itself somewhat didactic (a truism perhaps just as well overlooked in this context).

For the sake of the human interest involved, it should be added that at the time of original writing of this essay, my employer, Central State University in Wilberforce, Ohio, was undergoing severe problems with drugs, owing to the disadvantaged background of much of the student body, but it was cited in the *Wall Street Journal* positively for having administered urine tests to make certain that incoming students were off hard drugs when they were admitted. Further, the administration received ample funds from the federal government to have special gates established at the various entrances to the campus so that potential drug peddlers would be disheartened from attempting to invade and upset this bastion of academia. The drug problem was and is a serious one indeed, and the relevance of "Kubla Khan" to such contemporary events can hardly be bypassed in the classroom.

Now although Coleridge himself was not addicted to opium at the time he wrote the poem (or composed it in his deep sleep or reverie, whatever it really was)—at least according to some Coleridgeans, though not all—his final stanza constitutes a curiously prophetic moral addendum insofar as his sickness thereafter produced a number of drug-related poems telling of the after-effects of the Rose of Love (notably "The Pains of Sleep") and led to his early death. Students would hardly miss such a point in class, the Romantic appeal of the poem notwithstanding, for its hidden innuendoes ("demon-" and "war") also forecast trouble in the offing. Yet attempts made to reach other teachers in a pedagogical article on the subject[2] were not taken seriously enough; in response, a colleague from another university parodied the approach in print with the saucy title "Hooked on English." But the point now is that if students are bound to be "hooked" on something, it would be better for them to sublimate their appetites through literature as long as it does not become an incentive (as with Burroughs' *Naked Lunch*) to further illicit experimentation.

The main purpose here is not, however, to justify a moralistic reading of the poem, for that would imply "reading into" it something that the author had not intended. Yet is there not evidence that Coleridge wanted the reader to think that the lyric was a fragment at least partly because its subject-matter, as well as the mode of composition behind it, was dangerous? Is not the implication present that if the reader dares to follow along the same lines he, too, may be adversely affected?

Such a hint is indeed evident, and reporting it may help students, if they have even a modicum of sophistication, to value the poetic prognostication. Ever since the discovery of the Crewe MS. (British Museum Add. MS. 50. 847), we have had an autograph copy of the poem with a number of readings which differ from those in the printed version. One of these (1. 16) is "Daemon Lover," a textual reading that has occasioned an article in *PMLA*.[3] (Although Professor Patterson prefers to find the meaning of *Daemon* positive, because that spelling was a common enough variant of *demon* its implications are still sinister.) Another textual reading that has not been pointed out as especially significant but which may be is in the very last line where the manuscript reads: "And drank the milk of Paradise" (not *drunk*). Coleridge evidently intended "drank" as a late eighteenth-century form of the past participle of "to drink." Thus he allowed for the ambivalence of "drank" being read also as a simple past form, one which is grammatically permissible here then as well.

What is especially intriguing is that the entry after "drank" as a past participle variant of "drunk" in the *Oxford English Dictionary* corroborates the proposed manuscript reading:

> ... from the 17th to 19th c. *drank* was intruded from the past tense into the past participle probably to avoid the inebriate associations of *drunk*.[4]

The circumstances in which Coleridge composed the poem suggest his self-consciousness in his use of the verb form and his decision to avoid connotations of having been unnaturally drugged. For pedagogical purposes at least, then, the MS version is superior to the printed text and may provide special insight into what was originally intended.

We may add a curious addendum. In a recent issue of *50 Plus*, a letter to the editor criticized an article which used the phrase "has never drank" as follows: "I always thought the past participle of *drink* was *drunk*, as in 'he on honeydew hath fed / And drunk the milk of Paradise.'"[5] The editor quickly apologized but added amusingly, "The use of 'drunk' by Coleridge is considered archaic today. The whole subject is giving us a hangover." Presumably what Coleridge meant in the printed version was not really "drunk" in the past sense, but "hath ... drunk," which has an archaic helping verb, but that is scarcely what the letter-writer had in mind. In any event, the effect, in the light of the MS, is still amusingly paradoxical.

Notes

1. *Selected Essays, 1917–1932*, p. 122. This position seems greatly at odds with both the New Criticism and Deconstructionism, but it has the benefit of requiring literature to be understood in its historical context.

2. See Ch. VI. The original article was published in the *English Association of Ohio Bulletin*, 11 (Dec. 1970), 9–11.

3. Charles I. Patterson, Jr., "The Daemonic in *Kubla Khan*: Toward Interpretation," *PMLA*, 89 (1974), 1033–42.

4. See *OED*, "Drink," v^1.

5. Correspondence in the March 1987 issue, p. 100.

Chapter VI

"Pot Luck": Drugs and Romanticism

Alethea Hayter has concerned herself with some of the more cultivated literary minds of the last century apropos of narcotic drug-taking: Coleridge, De Quincey, Poe, Baudelaire and the Club des Haschischins, Collins, Thompson, Keats, and various others.[1] The Coleridgean case is particularly apropos since his "fragmentary" lyric "Kubla Khan" is very likely the world's most documented short poem (with the possible exception of a psalm) and was purportedly written under the influence of laudanum, a liquid form of opium mixed with alcohol. Does this purported fact, one that has been disputed, it may be asked, justify the *creative* use of narcotics? Let us investigate, metaphoric lens in hand.

A brief consideration of some recent research on this poem since George Livingston Lowes's epoch-making *The Road to Xanadu*, which was partly about this lyric and is sometimes called *the* scholarly study in source-hunting, can aid in determining the effect of opium on the creative imagination. Some time ago also, Meyer H. Abrams, one of America's leading specialists on English Romanticism, published an important Harvard essay on Romantic drug-addiction entitled *The Milk of Paradise*. Although his title obviously derives from the last words of "Kubla Khan," it also serves as a sort of justification for us to relate the term Rose of Love to the opium poppy. In short, if the drug itself can relate to "milk," why not the flower to the symbolic rose? In any event, Hayter referred to it as an indispensable work for the connoisseur, but taking issue with Abrams was notably Elizabeth Schneider, whose volume *Coleridge, Opium and "Kubla*

Khan" challenged the traditional view, upheld by Abrams, that the *effect* of the poem, aesthetically that is, may indisputably be traced to its *cause*, the taking of opium. In short, she denied that Coleridge composed the poem in a profound opium deep sleep, as he said in his Preface. She thus found him basically a prevaricator. Her view was upheld by numerous scholars, for example Marshall Suther, who in his *Visions of Xanadu* found the poet indebted to his own unconscious in other respects. But a study that gives more credence to Abrams's view is that by William B. Ober, one gracefully entitled "Drowsed with the Fume of Poppies: Opium and John Keats."[2] Ober contended that Keats wrote of water, for example, as purplish owing to the effects of opiate hallucination; the same may be said of the synaesthesia of the French *décadents*. Did not, then, Coleridge's own acquaintance with opium likewise enhance his creative product? (As for Keats, he simply used too little of it to be classified as an addict.)

In his turn, Geoffrey Yarlott has provided an answer. His book on "Kubla Khan" and Coleridge's related poetry as revealing hidden knowledge of the Romantic's life has to be read with care if only because it tends to confuse art with life, though it has useful insights.[3] Let us take his referring to T. S. Eliot's remarkable criticism that the poem is not really of superior quality because its imagery had not been "*used.*"[4] At first flush, such a disclaimer may appear ridiculous in that the enormous outpouring of scholarship on this so-called "Fragment" attests rather to its having been "used" very much indeed. But Eliot's adverse remark may also be of value in hinting at a *destructive* rather than merely inspirational effect of the narcotic. What he meant is that the imagery in the lyric was more or less set up side by side, as it came out, without real, purposeful organization. It reveals lack of inhibition, yes, but spontaneity is hardly enough. Where is the structure? In answer, many critics today favor the view that the form of the poem resides in its being *about* the writing of poetry. But perhaps that is too aestheticist to satisfy most readers.

Yarlott himself considered the poem as a case study in nineteenth-century hedonism, though he makes the following qualification:

> "Pleasure" was, in fact, a concept closely bound up with moral considerations for Coleridge: ideally, duty and pleasure should be synonymous but, in practice, this is seldom the case. Pleasure was not for him the same as "joy"—"there is joy above

Chapter VI: "Pot Luck": Drugs and Romanticism

the name of pleasure"—and joy demands the prior experience of God. Thus, pleasure pursued for its own sake, and devoid of moral or spiritual considerations, is a transitory thing, "unholy, frail and feverish."[5]

He then spent some pages reporting that Coleridge was by no means *impotent*, either creatively or biographically, as if pleasure and potency were somehow synonymous. What we may learn from this approach is that whereas an unrepentant narcotics addict may be guided by hedonism alone, a truly creative mind can see himself objectively and thus be led to moral adjudication. This search for moral conviction is recognizable at the end of "Kubla Khan," as I have already hinted at in the preceding chapter.

Toward the close of the poem, the speaker laments, "*Could* I revive within me ...";[6] for, alas, he cannot. His creative impoverishment, symptomatic of the aftermath of taking a narcotic, is clear in the final effects of the lyric. It is the *Khan* who *can*; the speaker, quite unlike the oriental potentate, *cannot*. The Khan decrees a pleasure-dome, hears ancestral voices prophesying war, and is the leader rather than the dreamer. Because, as Dorothy Wordsworth has informed us, Coleridge pronounced the name *Khan* the same as *can* (the words then sometimes being homophonic), the distinction between action and passivity is tantamount to the meaning of the poem. (Incidentally, I am indebted to F. W. Bateson, former editor of *Essays in Criticism* at Oxford and himself a noted Wordsworth scholar for bringing this phonological matter to my attention.) The question then is whether the speaker is debilitated through guilt feelings resulting from the partaking of a drug unnatural for human beings.

The answer is affirmative, though at the same time the speaker's ability to perpetuate his opium fantasy on paper was physically curtailed by the interruption of the famous visitor on business from Porlock. For even though Coleridge was against appending a moral to a work of art that should be judged aesthetically, his conservatism prevailed, and here he did so nonetheless. This reversion to a moral ending is true in "The Rime of the Ancient Mariner," though the moral there is aesthetic, not didactic, and it is true enough of "Kubla Khan," where the moral is, in effect, "Beware, beware of the perils of hedonism for its own sake."

What, we may ask, can be more symbolic of sheer pleasure than an exotic, erotic pleasure palace? And what can be more symbolic of its transitory nature than that it dissolves in the mind of the dreamer, cannot be recreated? The last few lines furnish a fitting caveat: they warn the reader that the fanciful poet-magician is not to be believed too literally, that the ordinary reader would "weave a circle round him thrice" and close his eyes with "dread." The reason given for this warning is that the speaker has "drunk the milk of Paradise," an action which is mystical enough, given the Edenic effect, but the sub-surface meaning, given the effects of opium, is that "he is drunk *on* this milk" or really narcotic. On the level of the initiation rite, the intrusion of the Porlock visitor serves as a convenient *deus ex machina* subtly and by implication instructing the reader that a very real possibility of moral intercession may be present in a moment of great sensuous temptation. (After all, among other exotic things, the Khan had a harem in his pleasure palace.) Man therefore is not to be tempted beyond his endurance. The Porlockian intrusion thus prevented Coleridge from further indulging in decadent hedonism, and his reflections on that produced the calculated end of the poem. We may think analogously of fate knocking at the door at the beginning of Beethoven's Fifth Symphony, or, more appositely yet, we might remember Edgar Allan Poe, intoxicated with alcohol no doubt, writing of the sudden tapping at the door in his popular poem "The Raven." Conscience acts like a quickened heart-beat, aesthetically represented by a rapping at the threshold.

Thus perhaps Nature has her own built-in defense mechanisms which may be more important to the truly creative mind than complete prohibition of narcotics in a free society. At any rate, this brief survey—corroborated by such Coleridgean buffs as Abrams, Hayter, and Yarlott—shows that even in the great Romantic poets, and especially in "Kubla Khan," the unnatural effects of opium can be dealt with as they should be: strictly. This attitude is easily corroborated through relating Coleridge's notable other opium dream poem "The Pains of Sleep," one which, though not so popular, has its title spelling out its central meaning.

Notes

1. *Opium and the Romantic Imagination* (Berkeley: University of California Press, 1968), passim.

2. *Bulletin of the New York Academy of Medicine,* 2nd ser., 44 (1968), 862–81.

3. *Coleridge and the Abyssinian Maid* (London: Methuen, 1967).

4. Cited by Yarlott, p. 127.

5. Yarlott, p. 131.

6. Line 42 (italics added).

Chapter VII

Byron's Bypath Back to Xanadu

The many attempts to map out the literary roadways to "Kubla Khan," commencing with John Livingston Lowes's seminal study *The Road to Xanadu*, have inadvertently obscured the memorable effect of this poem on subsequent poets who have themselves revealed a debt, one in turn to this most exotic of short lyrics. To adapt a familiar phrase, the Rose has come now full circle. Clearly the most likely Coleridgean influences of this nature would have been exerted during the later years of Romanticism, and indeed such a debt has been discerned in the later Wordsworth[1] and Tennyson.[2] Because, however, Coleridge announced prefatorily that "[t]he following fragment is here published at the request of a poet of great and deserved celebrity," by common consent Lord Byron, it is scarcely so odd to discern an "echo" or two of the Xanaduvian poem reverberating in this great literary lover's own most famous amorous work, *Don Juan*. Even a remote resonance of *Khan* in *Juan* may gladden the ear, albeit both names were commonly pronounced differently at that time. This essay will deal not with Byron's influence on Coleridge as posited by the latter, but with the reverse, then, in terms of the leading epical work aforementioned.

In Canto 1, stanza civ, the following Byronic lines indirectly but distinctively recall the final description of the Moorish damsel with her dulcimer:

> When Julia sate within as pretty a bower
>   As e'er held houri in that heathenish heaven
> Described by Mahomet, and Anacreon Moore,
>   To whom the lyre and laurels have been given,
> With all the trophies of triumphant song. . . .[3]

Instead of a dulcimer, she has a lyre, but she, too, is a songster and confined. The lines call to mind as well, and in a somewhat more specific textual manner, certain earlier ones in the Coleridge lyric: "as holy and enchanted / As e'er beneath a waning moon was haunted / By woman wailing for her demon-lover!" (14–16). For instance, the seemingly sacrilegious, or at least non-Christian, juxtaposition of "holy" and "enchanted" / "demon-lover" in Coleridge is akin in its exoticism to Byron's "heathenish heaven." On the purely verbal level, the simile in the former is set up precisely the same way as Byron's, the collocation "as ... / As e'er" happening to be present in both passages for what that may be worth. The overall effect is hardly earth-shaking, admittedly, but it is at least *Xanadu*-shaking, and that is all that counts at this point.

True, the plight of the earlier incarcerated dulcimer damsel derives partly, as is well recognized, from an Islamic "false paradise," as it is called, one described in *Paradise Lost*, to which "Kubla Khan," as is extremely well known, is substantially indebted in terms of some of its imagery. If Lord Byron does not subscribe to a Miltonic debt here as well, he still makes explicit use of the Moslem setting. The seeming, teasing discrepancy between dulcimer and lyre is actually more of a similarity when we garner all the facts. For did Coleridge really mean a dulcimer? As Hayter has shown, that instrument was usually taken to be a large "flat box up to three feet wide, standing on a table or on its own legs, most definitely not portable, and played with two hammers" (220). More likely he had in mind the older definition of *dulcimer* as recorded in the Bible, even if "we have no sure knowledge" of that,[4] but most probably he imagined the instrument as being somewhat like a lyre (certainly not an unportable box), and hence it would be akin to that mentioned by Byron.

In addition, Coleridge's notable penchant in this reverie-poem for correlating contraries (concave and convex in the caverns and dome, demonic and holy, sun and moon) related to a similar kind of fusion, although one more for rhetorically paradoxical and lightly facetious purposes, in the Byron passage. Consider the following: "The precipice she stood on was immense, / So was her creed in her own innocence" (cvi, 7–8) as well as the obvious *sun/moon* juxtaposition (cii, 4; ciii, 3). The attraction of opposites in terms of different races is suggested in both poems in this connection: Julia is a Moorish slave to love, presumably black, even as the Abyssinian

Chapter VII: Byron's Bypath Back to Xanadu

maid enacts a similar role in the Coleridge poem. On the archetypal level, these attractions of opposite magnetic poles, so to speak, bring to mind the Romantic sponsorship of the mysterious, dark-eyed, Middle Eastern beauty who also appears in Thomas Moore (to whom Byron refers in the quotation from *Don Juan*), Mary Shelley (Saphie in *Frankenstein*), and Keats (the Indian Maid in *Endymion*).[5]

At this point it is requisite to make a slight digression, reverting again to the precise pronunciation of Coleridge's title as reported by Dorothy Wordsworth. She claimed that he rhymed *Khan* with his end-sounds *ran* and *man* in the first stanza, as seems natural enough, yet that is not what was read aloud to me in the "official" reading of the poem at the bicentennial celebrations attending the anniversary of Coleridge's birth in the Lake District in 1972. Her statement testifying to this verdict is also in the report in her journals that she "carried *Kubla* to a fountain."[6] If, indeed, the Wordsworthian "drinking-*can* for use on journeys was playfully nicknamed after Coleridge's poem," as has been claimed,[7] then the name play on *Kubla* and *can* as homophonic with *Khan* is self-evident.

On the other hand, Elizabeth Schneider has felt that, in this context, "*Kubla*" was not an allusion to the reverie-poem after all; she argued that the lyric had to be composed later. For that unsettling view, she was challenged by Meyer Abrams, in his review of her book, and by J. B. Beer, who disassociated himself from her in his review of Suther's book.[8] Next, Jean Robertson, in published correspondence following the review by Beer,[9] ventured that Wordsworth's sister could have assimilated the German word *Kübel* (meaning milking-pail or bucket), particularly because she was sojourning in Germany at the time. That was ingenious, but what she failed to mention was that Dorothy might just as easily have alluded to the diminutive form *Kübele* or *Küb'le*, which would be even closer phonologically. Yet for that matter it would likewise relate to the Greek κυβελα, which means earth goddess and has been related in strong archetypal terms to this poem.[10] In any event, some question has been raised as to whether Dorothy knew enough German, let alone Greek, to make this association.

Whatever the case, such linguistic evidence would support wordplay also on the name of the potentate and thereby of the poem itself. Because she took her "*Kubla* to a fountain," it stands to good reason that she went there to secure fresh drinking water. It is likewise Romantically effective to imagine her taking a manuscript of the poem to be read by the fountain (one being also cited in the lyric) for atmospheric or tonal effect. Hence she would have readily dubbed her can *Kubla*, referring thereby to the *Khan* by pronouncing the word the same as *Can*, which was a common variant of *Khan* then anyway. In the process she could have whimsically associated the denotative Germanic resonance with a connotative allusion to the oriental ruler who happened to officiate also by a fast-paced gusher of water. Such a reading, however intense, is still of value because it helps vindicate the old theory that the poem was composed before October 1798,[11] when the Wordsworths came to Germany, and is indirectly thereby supportive of what Coleridge himself wrote.

Finally we can see just how this little digression (which also ties in with the last chapter and so serves as a transition too) ties in with Byron. We arrive at the intriguing possibility that he followed the same procedure as Coleridge did in rhyming "Khan" with "ran" and "man," when he pronounced the name of his own titular figure, Don Juan. With both poets, the sound is thus transformed to accommodate the exigencies of the other terminal sounds. It is plausible enough that Byron got the idea of Anglicizing the name from Coleridge having done so himself. At any rate, "Juan" rhymes with "Khan" throughout. That being probable, we might reasonably go a step further and think of Byron as thereby repaying his Romantic mentor, as it were, for the critical compliment graciously bestowed on him in the Preface to "Kubla Khan." Very likely the opium flower as the Rose of Love was responsible for more creativity in the earlier poem than modern skeptics have chosen to concede. As a symbol of the love for woman here expressed in various ways, wild and yet domestic (like the Jungian anima, for example, and symbolized in the wailing woman and then the dulcimer damsel), this flower would here assume the place of the more standard love rose, namely the blooming petals themselves.[12]

And, after all, if it first appears too informal for Dorothy Wordsworth to have referred to "Kubla Khan" in such an offhand manner (as "*Kubla*"), we have the precedent of Coleridge himself, who referred to the subject of his dream in the same manner in his poem (l. 29).

Notes

1. See Donald Ross, Jr., "*The Prelude, VIII*," *American Notes and Queries*, 5 (1966/67), 147–48.

2. See R. F. Fleissner, "Tennyson's Hesperidean Xanadu: The Anagogical Thread," *Research Studies* (Washington State University), 39 (1971), 40–46.

3. Reference is to *Byron's Don Juan: A Variorum Edition*, ed. T. G. Steffan et al., 4 vols. (Austin: University of Texas Press, 1957), II, 77.

4. According to Grove's *Dictionary of Music and Musicians*, 6 vols. (New York: Macmillan, 1937), II, 107, about such dulcimers "we have no sure knowledge."

5. I am indebted to Bruce E. Miller of SUNY Buffalo for reading an early draft of this paper and suggesting these additions.

6. *Journals of Dorothy Wordsworth*, ed. E. de Sélincourt—as cited by Elizabeth Schneider, *Coleridge, Opium and "Kubla Khan"* (Chicago: University of Chicago Press, 1953), p. 360. See especially her Appendix III, "Dorothy Wordsworth's 'Kubla,'" pp. 298–305. I am indebted to the late F. W. Bateson of Oxford University for personally bringing this matter of Coleridge's probable pronunciation, as based on Wordsworth's diaries, to my attention. It is also cited in J. B. Beer, *Coleridge the Visionary* (London: Chatto & Windus, 1959), p. 348, n. 59.

7. H. M. Margoliouth, *Wordsworth and Coleridge, 1795–1834* (Hamden, Ct.: Archon, 1966), p. 49.

8. *The Review of English Studies*, n.s. 18 (1967), 88.

9. Ibid., 438–39.

10. See Richard Gerber's "Keys to *Kubla Khan*," *English Studies*, 44 (1963), 322–23.

11. This early date is still good to hold on to. For an example of the absurdity that can result otherwise, cf. Michael Grosvenor Myer, "The Origin of a Phrase in *Kubla Khan*," *Notes and Queries*, n.s. 30 (1983), 219. Myer contends that reference to "Daemon Lover" in the Crewe MS. of the poem derives from Scott's ballad "The Daemon Lover," but that appeared in 1812. Hence Myer bases himself on the extraneous fact that the poem was *printed* only in 1816, whereas the MS was much earlier.

12. I have discussed the probability of Byron's being indebted to "Kubla Khan" briefly with Professor Thomas McFarland, the noted Princeton University authority on Coleridge, after his 1983 MLA talk on the poem. He was amenable to my suggestion in general, claiming, for example, that "*The Ancient Mariner* is the Bloomean 'strong precursor,' as it were, of *Don Juan*," not to mention *Childe Harold*. I cite him with his gracious permission. For further consideration of the debt of the Romantics to "Kubla Khan," see Northrop Frye, "The Drunken Boat: The Revolutionary Element in Romanticism," in *Romanticism: Points of View*, 2nd ed., ed. Robert F. Gleckner (Englewood Cliffs: Prentice-Hall, 1970), p. 308: "The 'Kubla Khan' geography of caves and underground streams haunts all of Shelley's language about creative processes."

Part III

Roses and "Modernism": (Stein, Frost, Eliot)— and Maugham

"The Rose where the Wounds of Christ are red"
—Edith Sitwell, *The Canticle of the Rose*

This final major section deals with three of the leading creative writers of modern times and their adoption of rose symbolism: Gertrude Stein, Robert Frost, and T. S. Eliot. Stein's often-cited shibboleth, "Rose is a rose is a rose is a rose," has become one of the most well-known *cris de coeur* in *avant-garde* literature, but, when considered in immediate context, actually also one of the most misquoted. In dealing next with Frost's manipulation of it for his own purposes, I shift from her use of four-fold roses to the latter's stress upon the next sequential digit, five. This shift was somewhat anticipated by Stein insofar as one variation of her familiar line already contains an extra rose: "Civilization began with a rose. A rose is a rose is a rose is a rose." In any case, the pentad is customarily linked with this flower, even as Taylor's *Encyclopedia of Gardening* describes it as "typically with 5 petals" at least in the wild, single variety, though "much more doubled in most horticultural forms."[1] Traditionally the number of petals involved has symbolic meaning; hence the seven-petaled rose is said to allude to "the septenary pattern," whereas the eight-petaled one "symbolizes regeneration."[2] Granted, Frost most probably was not conscious of this. That, however, is not exactly the issue here.

With Eliot, we focus on the "Multifoliate rose" and vacuity in "The Hollow Men." Although he could have known something of the Swiss psychologist Jung, especially when he was treated for stressful conditions in a Swiss sanatorium, his physician, Dr. Vittoz, is not on record for having been a Jungian. In any event, he allowed for critical interpretations of his poetry which went considerably above and beyond his own immediate or professed intent. Jungian interpretations of Eliot are hardly novel. Also relevant is the curious parallel that the phrase "hollow men" is already to be found in *Julius Caesar*, 4.2.23, and that other lines in the lyric are clearly traceable to that play (2.1.63–65); Eliot explicitly quoted these echoes in his Introduction to Paul Valéry's *Le Serpent*, as is well recognized. Thus, reference to "the Shadow" in this austere poem may allude not to the Christian conscience but the Stoic.

Finally I include a chapter on Somerset Maugham, though he is not a Modernist *per se*, because his more psychological use of rose symbolism ushers in a special case, one which will have to speak for itself.

Notes

1. Ed. Norman Taylor, 4th ed. (Boston: Houghton Mifflin, 1961), p. 1040.

2. J. E. Cirlot, *A Dictionary of Symbols*, trans. Jack Sage (New York: Philosophical Library, 1962), p. 263.

Chapter VIII

Four Roses and a Stein

The double meaning of the title warrants some explanation first. To begin, it has an initial literal meaning; the purpose of this essay is to come to terms with Gertrude Stein and her four roses:

Rose is a rose is a rose is a rose.[1]

Secondarily, the hint of alcohol in the title, even of a standard blended whiskey in a beer glass, is deliberately "absurdist": it is meant to show how her line gives the impression to some traditionally minded readers that she is needlessly repeating herself, that in effect such repetition is "absurd." By pure historical standards, it clearly is odd. Thirdly, and finally, the paper was composed between the end of one year and the first day of the next—hence rightly a period for seasonal cheer. But to revert to the "absurdist" suggestion, let us not proclaim a coming year a happy one by brandishing a stein of whiskey; instead let us momentarily consider the seeming nonsense in her line (only to prove it isn't). If Stein had celebrated at all, she would of course have easily quaffed a glass of wine in Paris ("With beaded bubbles winking at the brim") rather than downed a shot of Four Roses. In any case, our critical New Year's resolution flatly stated can be to find the meaning instead of the sting in Stein's poetic Four Roses.

To try to do so may seem defeatist from the start since, to many puritan readers, an analysis of such a short, repetitious line would appear to amount to a *tour de force*. Further, Archibald MacLeish's famous utterance, "A poem should not mean / But be," easily reverts to mind, encouraging the would-be critic to abstain from pressing a message from an object which is essentially aesthetic. Still, since poetry deals with words, and words (being quite different from, even if allied to, musical notes) are meant to communicate thoughts, an interpretation even of such an isolated line can be vindicated.

Truly Stein's four roses have had a decided impact upon twentieth-century poetry and criticism. Some of it has admittedly been negative, but mainly it has had its provocative effect. The very conciseness of the expression relates it to the popularity of other short poetic forms, notably the Japanese haiku and the brief statements of William Carlos Williams. Yet to come to terms with the meaning of the roses, certain fundamental questions must be asked and, at least in part, answered. The adverse criticism of the line cannot so easily be dismissed.

This criticism has usually taken the following form: the poetry is an example (or symbolic) of esoteric modern verse which fails to communicate to the average reader because it does not inform in a commonsense manner; it is aesthetic*ist*, not just aesthetic, in that it stands for the whole "*l'art pour l'art*" movement; indeed the very line itself would seem to "echo" the movement's name, suggesting meaningless repetition. Finally, from a logical standpoint the concept of the four roses is boring or, worse, dizzying, and, worst of all, tautological rather than, say, teleological in the Aristotelian sense.

Quite a lot to blame in such a short line. Granted, but the criticism does not stop there. The line has been attacked as affected. One of the better-known parodies reads as follows: "A pose is a pose is a pose."[2] The well-known light verse poet Richard Armour has suggested another variation: "She arose, she arose, she arose," meaning that she kept arising on different days or, better, kept getting up and then going back to bed again.[3] Perhaps the most cultivated expression of the reader's perplexed reaction to it is the following as cited in Malcolm Brinnin's *The Third Rose*: "I can go along with these first two roses of hers all right ... but when she gets to that third rose she loses me."[4] Brinnin's study is then confessedly an attempt to probe the essential significance of this third rose. The goal of this chapter is, paradoxically, even more ambitious: to ascertain what she had in mind with even the *fourth* rose.

It is helpful, as a starter, to examine what Stein herself had to say about this poetic line. As Howard Greenfield tells us in his

Chapter VIII: Four Roses and a Stein

biography, "Her method was a serious one, carefully thought out, yet she was too often made fun of. Thus, when at the University of Chicago, she was asked for the meaning ... she was glad to have a chance to explain clearly. . . ."[5] Part of her statement is worth citing here:

> Now you all have seen hundreds of poems about roses and you know in your bones that the rose is not there. . . . Now I don't want to put too much emphasis on that line, because it's just one line in a longer poem. But I notice that you all know it; you make fun of it, but you know it. . . . I think that in that line the rose is red for the first time in English poetry for a hundred years.[6]

Most likely she did not want to say more than the round number of a century so that she would still be giving credit to those famous rose poems before hers, probably Goethe's "Heidenröslein" and Robert Burns's "O my Luv's like a red, red rose." Burns was one of her favorites.

Her statement is of value for the record, especially because of its stressing that the rose is really *there*, but it does not actually say very much. Like much of her prose and poetry, the statement is essentially an expression of Primitivism. (She and Hemingway were key members of the "modernist" movement.) It is "primitive"—in the way Grandma Moses's paintings also are in their picturesque redundancies—to underscore the *thereness* of an object in poetry by merely reiterating the word. And her remark does not come to terms with the other criticisms she has received. Why, for instance, did she select a *rose* to repeat? Admittedly it is more charming than, say, a crass dandelion, but what makes it so special? The skeptic may still make fun of her by saying that all her line makes him think of is the worn-out, repetitious bromide "Business is business."

So, with not much help from Stein on the matter, let us find out for ourselves. One other remark of hers, uttered elsewhere, should be taken into account: that the original line has often been misquoted. She claimed that what she wrote was "Rose is ..." not "*A* rose is. . . ." In a word, she was talking about a woman called Rose and describing her in rather traditional terms, but emphasizing her beauty by underscoring the identification. The effect should be highly complimentary. In itself, this explanation seems very nice, if quaint, purely from a human point of view, but it is not yet fully satisfying to all tastes. We must bear in mind, moreover, that this qualification of hers ("Rose" for "A rose") has been set alongside other "variants" of her line. For instance, we might meditate on the following:

> Civilization began with a rose. A rose is a rose is a rose is a rose.[7]

Or take this one:

> Suppose, to suppose, suppose a rose is a rose is a rose is a rose.[8]

The last variant is then followed by wordplay on *arose* in the next line (as in the Armour parody). The effect seems more phonological than, if one likes, psycholinguistic, pointing again to the apparent "*l'art pour l'art*" quality of her verse, an effect that seemingly defies communicative meaning at times. It appears to be only play with words for the random sound combinations evoked. But we must remember that beauty is its own justification often enough, or it should be.

The interpretation now to be offered may seem heretical to some, especially to members of "the aestheticist school," but it at least clarifies the crucial line for the general reader. The point is that as many meanings can be found as there are roses. In other words, the line incorporates four basic rose meanings. These are, briefly, (1) the Impressionistic, (2) the technical, (3) the meaning of the rose itself, and (4) the anagogical.

The first is simple enough, implied already by Stein. Since Impressionism is a style that often is related to music (as in the poetry of Poe, who so strongly influenced the French Symbolists), her repetition exemplifies what might even be called a *Zeitgeist*, one which emerged in the late nineteenth century and was carried down into our own. Poe's "The Bells" is the best known example of this style, which is most effectively summed up in a recent biography of the poet, *Poe Poe Poe Poe Poe Poe Poe*.[9] Such a movement relates itself historically to aestheticism, of course, and if we wish to stay clear of the Dadaistic implications of this *fin de siècle* approach, let us accept the verdict that the Impressionistic or phonological effect of Stein's line can be enhanced through our reading it with different intonations (or tonal values) in terms of volume, pitch, and intensity. When the listener expects a different sound emanating from the reader (preferably a woman, though she hardly need be called Rose) with each mention of the word *rose*, he is charmed. For Stein has a hidden method for her "madness": "She does not believe, in spite of her reputation to the contrary, that Art is esoteric, Art for Art's sake, a thing removed from life having no practical function."[10]

The second meaning is the technical. Stein has been best known, aside from this line, for her experimentation with "automatic writing," most notably in *Three Lives*. This manner of composition, which involved her deliberately not looking at her page until she came to the end of it, no doubt contributes to her repetitive style. This is by no means the whole, or main, answer, but it ought not to be ignored by the sensitive critic, who must take into strict account the historical basis of a poem. Because in a very fundamental sense form cannot be wholly separated from content or meaning, the formal or technical side of her writing also has to be given its due.

The third meaning deals with her subject-matter. She chose such a flower because its very shape suggests the repetition of the word; the line conjures up the classical image of a rose with its interwoven petals. A memorable poetic line or phrase of her close friend T. S. Eliot easily comes to mind as an analogy (see Chapter XI): "Multifoliate rose." Perhaps, then, if a woman (Rose) is a multifoliate flower, she also has the layers of beauty and of mystery found in the roseate shape.

The fourth, and most important, is the mystical. With Stein being of Jewish extraction, it would be altogether fitting to discern an "echo" of the Scriptures in what she composed. Granted, her religion was not emphasized, but her father did attend synagogue services, "and the children for a time went regularly to Sabbath school."[11] Her coterie friendship with Eliot, whose religion became so very important to him and his writing, is undeniable. Because Eliot made so much of the rose symbol in *Four Quartets* and elsewhere, and since he was responsible more than anyone else for a revival of interest in Dante and the medieval rose symbol as stressed in the *Paradiso*, Stein certainly would have been aware of the import of the Mystical Rose. Exactly how she meant to transmit the image in her line is the question. The rose often has a Christian meaning, which presumably she would not have accepted, but she would have known of the Old Testament saying that the wilderness will "blossom as the rose." Most probably the influence of Scripture is best revealed in the most famous of all Talmudic phrases, one so important that it is regularly put in full capitals: "I AM THAT I AM." By adapting this phrase to suit a rose, she was showing how she, too, was created in God's image. In a word, her line is an aesthetic, perhaps Spinozistic, formulation of a religious or metaphysical statement (The Principle of Identity) on the nature of Jehovah, an equation that has been interpreted philosophically as "a Being whose Essence is His very Existence."

Of the different meanings presented for the quadruple roses, the last one would cap them all, but (to accommodate the definition just provided) let us conclude that although this resonance can be called the most "essential," given her twentieth-century milieu and Primitivistic proclivities, the other three meanings advanced above were also, at least, "existential."

Notes

1. From "Sacred Emily," in her *Geography and Plays* (Boston: The Four Seas, 1922), p. 187.

2. See Howard Greenfield, *Gertrude Stein: A Biography* (New York: Crown, 1973), p. 126.

3. In a private communication from Richard Armour.

4. John Malcolm Brinnin, *The Third Rose: Gertrude Stein and Her World* (Boston: Little, Brown, 1959), p. xiii.

5. Greenfield, pp. 126–27.

6. Greenfield, p. 128.

7. Brinnin, p. xi.

8. From "Syntax and Elucidation," in *A Primer for the Understanding of Gertrude Stein*, ed. Robert B. Haas (Los Angeles: Black Sparrow Press, 1971), p. 101.

9. Garden City: Doubleday, 1972. (The author is Daniel Hoffman.)

10. See Harvey Eagleson, "Gertrude Stein: Method in Madness," *Sewanee Review*, 44 (1936), 165.

11. Brinnin, p. 19.

Chapter IX

From Stein to Frost: The Germinal Soil of a Rose Family

> The rose is a rose.
> And was always a rose.
> But the theory now goes
> That the apple's a rose,
> And the pear is, and so's
> The plum, I suppose.
> The dear only knows
> What will next prove a rose.
> You, of course, are a rose—
> But were always a rose.
>
> —Robert Frost, "The Rose Family"[1]

As is generally recognized, Robert Frost's "The Rose Family" recalls intentionally Gertrude Stein's best-known line (but one so often misquoted), "Rose is a rose is a rose is a rose." Whereas misquoters frequently start off with "*A* rose is a rose," Frost rang a change on the line by commencing his lyric with "*The* rose is a rose." Many readers are led to believe that he was making fun of her, just as he lightly satirized other twentieth-century poets like T. S. Eliot and Archibald MacLeish. Yet we may find more meaningful petals to the Frostian flower, or more members in his rose family, than have hitherto been, say, supposed (to cite his rhyme perhaps also "borrowed" from Stein). For the poem has literary resonances that go beyond the obvious satire of Stein.

Still, initially it is useful to clarify the connection with the famous Stein statement. It is clear that he also had in mind her own gloss on the line, as formulated, according to Thornton Wilder, for one of her students: "I'm no fool; but I think that in that line the rose is red for the first time in English poetry for a hundred years."[2] (This version differs slightly from that given in the previous chapter, but may be a variant owing to a different occasion.) The comment is curious. The linking coordinating conjunction *but* can be taken in such a way as to make her meaning sound actually foolish. Although, in her remarks, she was evidently using hyperbole or a form of poetic license, it is also clear enough why Frost chose to parody her, even as he also made fun, to cite a prime analogy, of his poet-friend Edward Thomas in "The Road Not Taken."

Analogous parodies easily come to mind with other poets, for example Peter Viereck's take-off on Joyce Kilmer's "Trees" with the witty turnabout at the end: "Poems are made by trees like me / But only God can make a fool." Frost, however, was doing rather more than joshing Stein about her often-misquoted redundant definition. He was probably aware that she also composed some famous variants of the line, ones found in "Objects Lie on a Table," "An Elucidation," and "As Fine as Melanctha."[3] His own wordplay on the rose as a feminine symbol points to his recognition that Stein had initially in mind not the flower *per se*, but a woman called Rose. Thus, he concludes in a characteristically gracious manner: "You, of course, are a rose— / But were always a rose."[4] Hence humor is overcome by grace. His earlier fond reference to Stein ("The dear only knows / What will next prove a rose") is both a playful gloss upon her making simply another rose prove a rose and upon her apologia ("I'm no fool; but ..."). His final reference ("You") is not to her, or her Rose, but to the reader.

Now let us consider other progenitors of this rose family. To take the poem on its most literal level and assume that the only family members are botanically the rose, apple, pear, and plum (not to mention the addressee) is superficial and overlooks the improbability that Frost had merely Stein in the back of his mind. Stein herself, however, was certainly well aware of the different resonances of her rose symbol, as suggested in the preceding chapter, and Frost ought to have been too. When she reflected that the rose has not been truly red for an entire century, we should look not at the time gap alone but at what immediately preceded it. She

Chapter IX: From Stein to Frost

evidently meant since the time of another Robert, namely Burns, whose familiar lyric commencing "O my Luv's like a red, red rose" appeared in Frost's favorite vade mecum, Palgrave's *Golden Treasury*. Frost's own Scottish background on his mother's side was evidently influential in making him particularly acclimatized to the poetry of Burns (as his brief tirade on the subject with T. S. Eliot, noted by Thompson,[5] assures us). Indeed, when he recited his poetry at the University of North Carolina at Chapel Hill, he was quaintly enough referred to, in a Burnsian manner, as Bobby Frost, albeit in that context the nickname might have been a bit condescending.[6] At any rate, in "The Rose Family" Frost meant to recall not only Stein but indirectly the poet to whom she was alluding, namely Burns. So more members are added to the family.

Another member, one who hides in the background but whose import is technically greater than that of either Stein or Burns here, is Austin Dobson. For Frost's poems shows marked connections with Dobson's "Urceus Exit," which is included in that other favorite anthology of Frost's, one that rivals Palgrave's *Golden Treasury*, namely the *Oxford Book of English Verse*:

> I intended an Ode,
>   And it turn'd to a Sonnet.
> I began *à la mode*,
> I intended an Ode,
> But Rose cross'd the road
>   In her latest new bonnet;
> I intended an Ode;
>   And it turn'd to a Sonnet.

Offhand, parallels may not appear very close, but the four-beat line, the unorthodox rhyme scheme, the short form, and the switching of the subject at the end are all related. Dobson's shift in the triolet from one topic to another is analogous to what Stein and Frost say has been happening to literary roses, and the explanation for the changeover is likewise abrupt, amusing, and with a touch of *cherchez la femme*. As Frost put it in his essay "The Constant Symbol," Dobson had "a better excuse for weakness of will than most, namely Rose."[7] He analyzed parts of the poem in this essay. Although her point has been largely given short shrift, Babette Deutsch recognized this affinity in her review when "The Rose Family" was published, calling it a verse "which might have been written by Austin Dobson in his sleep."[8] Because the Dobson poem, originally written under the rubric of "Rose-Leaves," has been considered one of the few successful triolets in English, it could well have interested the technician in Frost on those grounds alone. Frost's originally designated biographer, Robert S. Newdick, also wrote of the New Englander's fondness for Dobson.[9]

In sum, then, the genealogy of "The Rose Family" includes first Dobson (the serious influence), next Stein (the object of the satiric or parodic element), and lastly Burns (the Romantic connection). Frost's imagery has more roseate significance than has hitherto been admitted.

Notes

1. Frost's lines are quoted with the permission of the Frost Estate but from the unmodernized text, *Complete Poems of Robert Frost* (New York: Holt, Rinehart and Winston, 1967), p. 305. Permission has also been obtained from Holt, Rinehart and Winston.

2. From the introduction to Wilder's *Four in America*—as cited by J. M. Brinnin, "Gertrude Stein in America," *The Atlantic Monthly*, 204 (October 1959), 99.

3. See R. Bridgman, *Gertrude Stein in Pieces* (New York: Oxford University Press, 1970), p. 139. These variants help to explain (though they scarcely condone) the misquotation of "Rose" as "A rose," as, for example, in Greenfield, p. 54.

4. Thus a choice example of a poem of Frost's that has started in delight and ended in wisdom, as he liked to have it.

5. Lawrance Thompson, *Robert Frost: The Years of Triumph, 1915–1938* (New York: Rinehart and Winston, 1970), pp. 402–3.

6. This is a recollection of my graduate school days. Frost spoke at Chapel Hill because he was a close friend of Professor Clifford Lyons there.

7. The essay appeared in *The Atlantic Monthly* (1946) and is reprinted in *Selected Prose of Robert Frost*, ed. Hyde Cox and Edward Connery Lathem (New York: Holt, Rinehart and Winston, 1966; rpt. Collier Books, The MacMillan Co., 1968), p. 28.

8. "Poets and Poetasters," *The Bookman*, 68 (1928), 471–72; rpt. by Linda Wagner, in *Robert Frost: The Critical Reception* (New York: Franklin, 1977), p. 69.

9. See *Newdick's Season of Frost: An Interrupted Biography of Robert Frost*, ed. William A. Sutton (Albany: State University of New York Press, 1976), p. 238. Thompson's two-volume biography does not cite Dobson, nor does the Thompson-Winnick third volume.

Chapter X

Sub Rosa:
Focussing on Frost's Flower as "Five-Petaled"

> "I am a mystic. I believe in symbols."
> —Robert Frost

Frost's functional use of the pentad as a subliminal structural device represents one of the underlying subtleties of his poetry only recently discerned. His accommodation of this key number in the history of Neo-Pythagorean lore is evident, for example, in "The Gold Hesperidee";[1] this has been corroborated in a major talk of his, one transcribed for the first time for the Frost centenary, during which he elaborated on the meaning of pentameter rhythm, the kinship of poetry to arithmetic and number in general, during which he named a key mathematician *en passant* and even deigned to designate the affinity as "very deep."[2] Memorably he chose to repeat the symbolic digit *five* nine times in a short paragraph (as the speech was published), citing precisely "five things to be done with a poem" in the process.[3] It is worthwhile to consider now whether such use of number had aesthetic significance for him elsewhere as well.

Let us, in answer, first turn to other poetry of his to consider evidence of possible pentad patterns or, as is usually said by Neo-Pythagoreans, "pentagonal symmetry." For example, in "'Out, Out—'" the mountain ranges number five, and although they symbolically relate to the buzz saw mentioned ("a jagged-tooth, saw-edge against the sky"), they also point to the five fingers of the hand being pathetically dismembered.[4] Because such a dire numerical correlation may not appear especially inviting to contemplate, we may consider it most probably neither consciously nor even unconsciously present; it can only be "read in." Still, in his so-called rigmarole poem, "The Rose Family," a rather more striking use of the pentad is noticeable. Since its formal arrangement has not been fully dissected yet (with apologies to Wordsworth), it deserves closer inspection now. In the previous chapter we have considered only its sources.

At the outset, the overall pattern bears more than, let us say, pictographic resemblance to William Carlos Williams's experimental poem of approximately the same length entitled "The Great Figure." The Williams construct was, of course, deliberately based on the pentad and in rather more than merely a titular capacity. First, it was occasioned by Charles Demuth's picture of an enormous number five painted in fire-engine red; secondly, the poem pivots structurally around clusters of five units.[5] Because Williams's verses in general have the same sort of short patterns, such a diagrammatic analysis may at first appear hard to prove; however, it can be well substantiated by the poem itself when aided by the familiar psychological truism that the mind is able to take in, at the most, five units at one time as a *Gestalt* and even that the natural affinity for this number may be based on the rods and cones in the eye. The Williams piece elevates our comprehension of the pentad's poetic role meaningfully, but admittedly its seeming "pop" effect lends itself to a somewhat low-keyed or merely impressionistic critical appreciation. The point is that "The Rose Family" may serve our purposes better, for it probes a bit more deeply into human understanding of Nature and thence the universe.

For a starter, in his helpful initiatory comment on the Frostian "family," a leading critic has tried to rehabilitate the seemingly frail lyric, generally dismissed as little other than the "rigmarole" Frost modestly termed it, by appropriately showing how "the form of the poem supports its content,"[6] but he did not go far enough. He did argue for the clear-cut debt to Burns and Stein, as independently posited in the last chapter, though he missed Dobson. He observed the fairly self-evident effect that "all ten lines" (note the number, which more than coincidentally happens to be a multiple of five) "end in the same rhyme sound," thereby emphasizing "the unity of rose, apple, pear, plum, and lady as all members of one 'family'": the

Chapter X: Sub Rosa

botanical *Rosaceae* as applied by analogy to the human species. In appraising such a "rigmarole," he noted that "the basic meter—anapestic dimeter—is gracefully suitable for the subject, and is skillfully varied." True enough, but let us carry such formal decipherment further. Notice that the count of the new "botanical" arrangement is five, that the average sum of words per line turns out to be five, that even the number of words in the title when conjoined with those in the name of the author is five. (This last addition is relatable as one extrinsic to the body of the poem itself.) The Frost concordance, moreover, confirms that his use of this centralized digit (that is, being significantly halfway between one and ten) is prominent enough throughout his poetry when compared with other numerals (excluding the common first three). Skeptics will contend that this sort of computation can be done with almost any number, but that is more easily said than done. When Frost's pentad accommodations affect his rose subject, at any rate, the result is, metaphorically, a "standard" five-petaled flower.

Are we not reminded of John Donne's charming poetic bouquet, "The Primrose"? There again a specifically feminine application of the pentad becomes structurally germane:

> Live Primrose then, and thrive
> With thy true number five;
> And women, whom this flower doth represent,
> With this mysterious number be content;
> Ten is the farthest number; if half ten
> Belong unto each woman, then
> Each woman may take halfe us men.
> (ll. 21–27)[7]

Again consider the structure. Although only three out of seven lines in the stanza are composed of five words each, other clusters are discernible upon close reading; in both the third and fifth lines, clusters of five words follow and precede the pointing; the fourth line contains ten syllables (a multiple of five). The same sort of structure is evident in the Williams poem and, as we shall see, in Frost's.

Was the number five in some way also the "true number" for Frost that it was for Donne? For what it may be worth, like the name Donne, Frost's own name contains the requisite number of letters, even as do those of Burns and Stein, quaintly enough. (Dobson's is also pretty close.) But such onomastic association is fairly minor, at least when compared with the intrinsic meaning the pentad might have had for Frost. Let us examine that philosophic basis now.

It seems likely that he was very possibly acquainted with the clustering in "The Primrose" if only because of Donne's having become so prominent, particularly after Eliot stressed the leading Metaphysical's import for modern times. Elsewhere Frost's apparent use of Donne's famous poem "A Valediction: forbidding Mourning" in his "Moon Compasses" has been explored;[8] the "imitation" may have been partly owing to the general influence of Eliot—Donne being "in the air" then for that reason.[9] What was of prime import was Donne's being *Metaphysical*, hence representing a philosophic stance that went significantly beyond the mere sense perception articulated in Petrarchan imagery. But Frost would have gone farther back to Donne in this respect. He was most probably well aware of the historically notable application of pentad lore for similarly well-stated Marian purposes in *Sir Gawayne and the Grene Knight* as evident in the prominent use of the pentangle on the hero's shield and the ensuing discussion of its meaning. On the same grounds, he also was no doubt keenly aware of Chaucer's ironic use of the same number, again partly for Marian purposes among others, in describing the five-times-married Wife of Bath.[10] Since he was a professed classicist (like Eliot again), he could have known of the Roman precedent for the Marian figure in Plutarch's *De E Apud Delphum* ("E" being the fifth letter), a point made by one of the leading contemporary numerologists, Alastair Fowler, when he was a Visiting Professor at Frost's Bread Loaf School of English.[11]

True, Frost may not have thought a great deal about the Catholic association of the pentad with the Five Wounds of Christ or the rosary (The Five Joyful, Five Sorrowful, and Five Glorious Mysteries) or with Mary's month (May) being the fifth. Such medieval, esoteric connections with Christian Neo-Pythagoreanism would easily have struck him as superstitious, though he showed some interest himself in Catholicism at Bread Loaf, and his daughter Lesley was later converted to the Roman church.[12] In any event, he would still have been very likely aware of the anagogic commonplace stemming from Dante and medieval tradition whereby the Virgin was venerated as the Mystical Rose. Again the meaning of the celebrated flower emerges as significant. As is well known, Frost utilized Dante's rhyme scheme from the *Commedia* for "Acquainted with the Night." Once more, for what it is worth, at least to round out the earlier onomastic proposal, the Florentine's surname again comprises the requisite number of letters. If some special pleading seems involved here, let us envision the numerical correlations as simply being too obvious to be farfetched. Granted they would not occur easily to the ordinary *casual* reader, but who wants to be limited to such dullness? Or to such a limited, pedestrian approach?

Let us therefore scrutinize the line-by-line structure of "The Rose Family" in factual terms and as circumspectly as possible. The poet already provides the hint in reminding us that "The fact is the sweetest thing that labor knows" (see his "Mowing"). So now we notice that the first four lines duly consist of five words each, the next two of a composite, six and four; the following two of a reversal of these, four and six. These average out to five apiece again. This structure is clearly elementary enough to be grasped by the common reader, when he is informed of it, at a glance (or even upon first hearing), so Frost could have meant it that way. Only the ninth line goes beyond the requisite bounds established, but for its own rather valid reasons, as we shall see. Finally, the tenth line encloses the little lyric, rounding it off with none other than five magical words. The use of the same end-rhyme throughout lends itself harmoniously to what might best be welcomed as a multi-petaled roseate appearance.

So why then the seemingly anomalous length of the ninth line? Evidently, aside from the need for avoiding the tedium of *complete* symmetry, because it is the most emphatic, needing more words to express itself: "a strong stress on the initial 'You' signals the 'turn' of the poem from the general to the personal."[13] Fine, but let us add that the dash at the end conveniently provides an open-ended effect (reminiscent of the ending of "Moon Compasses"), thus making the exact count of the words in this simple instance relatively unimportant. This very exception proves the rule, as it were, for the neglect of the roseate principle for just one moment has the effect of calling attention to it elsewhere. We recall easily enough the commonplace that a woman may be perfect in every respect but one: she can have a slight disorder in the dress, in her manner of speech, or habits, which makes her attractive for that very reason. The meaning of the female presence of [R]ose in the poem becomes relevant.

On another level, the lack of symmetry in the ninth line conveys a deeper meaning: thematically it reaches out to embrace love and not only in the human but divine sense. At first flush, such a seemingly "prettified" reading may seem like overdoing it, since divinity has so often been associated in human understanding with conformity and formality. But, Romantically, that criterion is not always the case, and in spite of Frost's claimed dissociation from Romantic escapism, he owed a considerable legacy to it. The Romantic understanding of God operative in Nature has its bearing here. Whereas Nature, as proponents of the Golden Proportion have shown,[14] conforms excitingly enough to the essentials of pentagonal symmetry (duplicated then in music, sculpture, architecture, and the fine arts in general), love clearly moves beyond computation as such when it reaches out for the Infinite.

As a final coda, let us observe that, as noted elsewhere,[15] it will not do to make a very strong case for Frost as a literary numerologist *per se.* He was not concerned with such an arcane stance. The bearing of the pentad upon several of his poems, most notably and obviously perhaps "The Rose Family," relates more to a classical formulation (only by derivation Pythagorean) of the Golden Mean Proportion. Such a view in the end turns out to be based on Nature more than simply occult. As with Frost's poem, rather more than mere "rigmarole" is involved.

Notes

1. See R. F. Fleissner, "Like 'Pythagoras' Comparison of the Universe with Number': A Frost-Tennyson Correlation," *Frost: Centennial Essays I,* ed. Jac L. Tharpe (Jackson: University Press of Mississippi, 1974), pp. 207–20.

2. For a transcription of the poet's talk of 27 July 1960, see Reginald L. Cook, ed., *Robert Frost: A Living Voice* (Amherst: University of Massachusetts Press, 1974), p. 159 especially.

3. Cook, pp. 150–51. For an analysis of Frost's speech in connection with his use of Tennyson (also cited in his talk), see R. F. Fleissner, "Frost and Tennyson: Factual as Well as 'Archetypal,'" *American Notes and Queries,* 14 (Dec. 1975), 53–55.

4. See William S. Doxey, "Frost's 'Out, Out—,'" *The Explicator,* 29 (April 1971), item 70.

5. R. F. Fleissner, "Homage to the Pentad: Williams' 'The Great Figure,'" *Notes on Contemporary Literature,* 1 (Sept. 1971), 2–6. (The

Chapter X: Sub Rosa 97

accompanying diagram, however, which I was not given to check in page proof, was somewhat misconstrued by the editorial staff.) For considerably more on this matter, consult Michael North, "The Sign of Five: Williams' 'The Great Figure' and Its Background," *Criticism,* 30 (1988), 325–48.

6. See Laurence Perrine, "Frost's 'The Rose Family,'" *The Explicator,* 26 (January 1968), item 43.

7. From *The Poems of John Donne,* ed. H. J. C. Grierson (Oxford: Oxford University Press, 1912), pp. 61–62.

8. R. F. Fleissner, "Frost's 'Moon Compasses,'" *The Explicator,* 32 (May 1974), item 66. Frost's poem, as well as Donne's (I presume), was dedicated to his spouse. In what turned out to be an all-too-cavalier survey of current Frost scholarship, a Vermonter took me to task by apparently challenging my suggestion that the last three dots in the Frost poem can be construed as playful ellipsis for "as with Donne." See Charles T. Morrissey, "The Poet and the Pedants," *The Chronicle of Higher Education,* 26 Feb. 1979, "Point of View" section. I did not, however, originally deny that the concluding periods may conventionally be taken as Romantically open-ended, but observed merely one valid imaginative replacement for the ellipsis.

9. It is possible that Frost was "copying" Donne also in imitation of T. S. Eliot, even as, for example, his close friend Dr. (Rabbi) Victor Reichert has privately communicated to me that "Directive" might be taken as a Frostian *Waste Land.*

10. R. F. Fleissner, "The Wife of Bath's Five," *The Chaucer Review,* 8 (1974), 50–54. See also my consideration of analogous use of the pentad as symbolic of marriage in "Goethe's Pentad and the Count," *Germanic Notes,* 12 (1981), 39–40. Again, observe that Frost's own work had a specifically marital meaning.

11. In a private communication of Professor Fowler's to me at Bread Loaf.

12. In a private communication at Bread Loaf, I heard of Frost's one-time interest in seeing a Jesuit priest, and I likewise heard of his daughter's conversion to Catholicism (through a granddaughter).

13. See n. 6 above.

14. Matila Ghyka, *The Geometry of Art and Life* (New York: Sheed and Ward, 1946), passim. The number five is basic to golden section proportionality (what Luca Pacioli termed *la divina proportione*), for it

relates to the regular pentagram based on Euclidean construction in terms of division into extreme and mean ratio. Most recently this divisionism has also been applied to T. S. Eliot. See Mildred Meyer Boaz,"'You Are the Music': Tuning in to Eliot," in *Approaches to Teaching Eliot's Poetry and Plays*, ed. Jewel Spears Brooker (New York: The Modern Lang. Assn., 1988), p. 65.

15. See n. 1 above.

This essay is dedicated in loving memory to Reginald L. Cook.

Chapter XI

Plucking at T. S. Eliot's "Multifoliate Rose" and Hollowness

The question is whether "the stuffed men" of Eliot's famous lament, once meant as an addendum to *The Waste Land*, are symbolic of a nihilistic attitude or whether their hollowness mainly represents an emptiness waiting to be filled. Presumably the latter attitude entails a potentiality for spiritual grace. Because the most recent comment on this controversy, which originally appeared in the leading professional journal on literary matters in America,[1] finds the difference a mere quibble,[2] a word should be said in favor of the time-honored, psychological distinction between the conception of nothingness *per se* and "hopeful emptiness," for the latter has some bearing on the key line or phrase "Multifoliate rose."

Because of Eliot's having suffered a breakdown and having even been treated in a Swiss sanatorium, we have some reasonable basis for considering his abstract poetry from the perspective of the leading Swiss psychologist, Carl Jung. Insofar as *The Waste Land* has come in for Jungian analysis, so might "The Hollow Men." The titles alone suggest an affinity, though perhaps not in themselves any sign yet of hope. Hence because of reference to the former poem in a standard handbook on Jungian psychology, one used as a guide for Jungian analysts in Switzerland, namely J. E. Cirlot's *A Dictionary of Symbols*,[3] it is helpful to return to the same work in terms of understanding the latter poem.

Cirlot has relevant material on the significance of both *Hollow*[4] and *Emptiness*.[5] The first entry relates the quality of being hollow to abstractions like "the Dead," "Memories," and "the past." These notions are clearly evident in "The Hollow Men" in such lines as "In *death's* dream kingdom," "Those who have crossed / With direct eyes, to *death's* other Kingdom / *Remember* us—if at all—not as lost / Violent souls, but only / As the *hollow* men / The stuffed men." Hints of "the past" are also found in such "echoes" of the past as "*Here we go round the prickly pear*," which is an obvious transformation of the nursery rhyme on going 'round the mulberry bush, and "*For Thine is the Kingdom*," which derives from the standard Protestant conclusion to the Lord's Prayer. One main *memory* of *the past* in terms of something *dead* (or inanimate), thereby combining all three abstractions, is another recollection of the nursery chamber: Eliot's appropriation of his central image from the talking Scarecrow of *The Wizard of Oz* and Baum's other books on the fanciful subject. Literally speaking, "stuffed men" would point to such conversing scarecrow figures first of all. Eliot is on record for having delighted in these children's stories, recalling, for instance, the Nome King of Oz much later in life for a friend.[6]

Granted, such a fairy-tale connection tells us little in itself about the spiritual import of "The Hollow Men," except maybe that their nihilism should not be taken too seriously. For this purpose, Cirlot's comments on the term *Emptiness* are especially apropos: "This is an abstract idea, the antithesis to the mystic concept of 'Nothingness' (which is reality without objects and without forms yet nurturing the seed of all things)."[7] Reference is then made to oriental religion, specifically Egyptian lore, and since Eliot appropriated even Sanskrit and both Buddhist and Hindu faiths in *The Waste Land*, its accommodation to "The Hollow Men" is comprehensible. In a word, regardless of how one wants to understand the concept of a void (whether in oriental terms as a vacancy or as sheer nihilism), a philosophic and psychological difference is manifest between this idea and that of waiting to be filled. It may be too strong to call such potentiality the direct "antithesis" to that of nothingness in this poem, but the conscientious reader should be able to see for himself a distinction that is not too subtle. The very notion of conscience may be symbolized in the lyric as "the Shadow," especially if the idea derives from Brutus's introspectiveness in *Julius Caesar*, as has often been thought (but that is another level).

Returning to Cirlot on the meaning of *Hollow*, we find him seeing the abstraction specifically in terms of "the unconscious" and what he designates "the mother" image. True, it is a bit difficult to find this further development in "The Hollow Men," particularly when "Lips that would kiss" only "Form prayers to broken stone." A religious hint of *Mater Dei* may, however, appear in the "Multifoliate rose" image, for Eliot was well acquainted with Mary's being called the Mystical Rose in Dante, and her veneration could then be "The hope only / Of empty men" who need her intercession. Let *us* hope also that what has been "plucked at" can finally be grasped.

Notes

1. Friedrich W. Strothmann and Lawrence V. Ryan, "Hope for T. S. Eliot's 'Empty Men,'" *PMLA*, 73 (1958), 426-32; also see 75 (1960), 635-38.

2. Robert H. Canary, *T. S. Eliot: The Poet and His Critics* (Chicago: University of Chicago Press, 1982), pp. 200-01.

3. Cirlot, pp. 160-61.

4. Cirlot, p. 143.

5. Cirlot, pp. 92-93.

6. See my piece entitled "Scarecrow Men" in *American Notes and Queries*, 7 (1969), 151; ibid., 8 (1970), 89-90.

7. Cirlot, pp. 92-93.

Chapter XII

A Rose Window on *Human Bondage*: An Overview of Its Onomastics

With the imposing name of W. Somerset Maugham being on record for having creatively transformed several key place-names in his leading, semi-autobiographical novel, *Of Human Bondage*, more detailed onomastic study is warranted. (This chapter ties in with the earlier one dealing with onomatological, personal allusions in *As You Like It*, though here the Rose specifically involved turns out to be male rather than female.)

Even as Maugham's invented town of *Blackstable* derives, in complementary fashion, from his Kentish upbringing in *Whitstable*— the creation of *Tercanbury* being similarly a flat reversal (of initial syllables in *Canterbury*)—the principal characters' names, too, convey appropriate meaning and are thus not merely "representative" ones reflecting regional locale and time.[1] To scout these possibilities, I have visited Whitstable, consulted the library and a local antiquarian, and have uncovered some new information, particular apropos of Dickens's visits to Whitstable, and his writings thereon, for Maugham was undoubtedly inspired in this novel by the Inimitable, as Dickens is so often acclaimed by his devotees.

Unlike the names originated by his contemporary Arthur Conan Doyle, Maugham's should be understood as rather more than popular labels accommodated freely from a telephone directory. Because, like so many modern novelists, he composed in the popular wake of Dickens, we well recall that his predecessor was already an expert in applying apt nomenclature to his characters, albeit more imaginatively. In any event, if, as Graham Greene once said, "Doyle's mastery of names is 'perhaps equalled only by Dickens,'"[2] rather more can now be said of Maugham's. Sir Arthur himself once admitted, "I give way to no-one in my admiration for that great man" (namely Dickens), but then he had to concede, by way of circumspect qualification, that if the Inimitable "had dropped all the Turveydrops and Tittletits and the other extraordinary names he gave to people, he would have made his work more realistic...."[3] Dickens, on the other hand, was actually concerned more with what is presently called *surrealism*; witness George Orwell's well-known volume on *Dickens, Dalí and Others*. Although, true enough, in *The Summing Up*, Maugham in fact found Trollope more "realistic" than Dickens (and thus would have sided with Doyle), he still owed a considerable legacy to Britain's most widely read former storyteller of repute; in *Books and You*, he dubbed him resolutely "England's greatest novelist," adding that "there is nothing to be said but that [*David Copperfield*] is Dickens' best novel," even if only because "his defects are here least noticeable and his merits most remarkable."[4] Yet the compliment is not merely back-handed.

The point is that Maugham's use of Dickens, particularly *Copperfield*, reveals one of the choice biographical influences which ultimately helped determine the overall shape of his writing style. He was much influenced by Dickens's "Whitstable connection," as it has been called,[5] in that he was aware of how the Inimitable and his cronies, such as Mark Lemon, visited the Whitstable area, including "The Golden Slipper," an entertainment spot, and knew of where Dickens resided in the oyster resort proper. It is not for nothing that one of Maugham's leading biographers has observed that his subject "in many ways, is to the twentieth century what Charles Dickens was to the nineteenth."[6] One obvious difference, naturally, is that Maugham did not have Dickens's genius. In any event, analyzing *Bondage* with Dickens in mind hardly offers too much of a surprise; it could even prompt or effect another kind of bondage, as it were, by helping us to tie together otherwise divergent aspects of autobiography, character, and theme. Thus, Maugham's use of Dickens emerges provocatively enough in counterpoint with his debt to his own personal background.

Philip Carey, the bondaged hero, reveals a bland enough cognomen, yet one which also heralds his gradual maturation and self-development as artist type and later physician. In courting such subtextual onomastic meanings, many of which were probably

Chapter XII: A Rose Window on Human Bondage

subliminal, a certain temptation to over-etymologize may be present, if only because many novelists admittedly do not so very deliberately load their characters' names with a vast amount of semantic or associative freight; however, it is still rather puzzling to know at times where to draw the line in purely aesthetic terms. What we are concerned with here primarily is valid connotation rather than etymology as such. At times such implication "works" in its fictional context; at other times it does not. But in all cases what is at stake is art more than life, and the art involved, if seemingly exaggerated, is that way partly because of the Dickensian onomastic connection.

For example, would not *Philip*, the Christian name, already convey a suggestive ambivalence? In at least nominally "echoing" that of an Apostle, it paradoxically also summons up secularly the Greek for *love* (*phileo*), and we momentarily think of the rose symbol again. The hero's personality is riven between an austere religious upbringing (his uncle being the stern Victorian minister type) and carnal love. Thus duality is already prefigured in the novel's title, deriving, as the Preface alerts us, from the *Ethics* of Spinoza, the pantheistic Jewish philosopher whose mystical influence upon a key cultural luminary like Goethe, who is duly cited in the novel, had been prominent. On the mystical level, then, Maugham's original working title, *Beauty for Ashes*, is also germane to the meaning in Philip's name, implying as it does that "aesthetics transcends death." The saying is a striking motto in context, deriving from Isaiah 61.3. Because Spinoza had vitally stirred Goethe's psyche, it is hardly inconsequential that the latter sage is cited in the Heidelberg section of the book. As *The Summing Up* assures us, his overall effect on Maugham was fairly memorable; he crops up again in *Books and You* (53-54). For, being an acute observer of his age, he had been a fellow student of human bondage, though in culturally a rather more universal sense. He thereby earned the title of the first true European, invented the term *Weltliteratur*, associations which Maugham took advantage of in his novel.

As to the overall "human" context of the book's final title, Maugham's general acquaintance with hebraic thought is of value, too, insofar as it permitted responsible agnosticism (owing ultimately to a Jehovah thought to be ineffable). Hence, Judaism has tolerantly allowed for accountable free thinking, the testing of ideas not only intuitively but socially and practically in terms of the crucible of experience, and of this liberal tendency Maugham was surely aware. Such experimental give-and-take runs over into *Bondage*, as the title already would imply, helping to explain its continuing appeal to young people.

Philip's name, however, implies more than what has thus far been proposed; it points back to the Greek for *horse-lover* (*philippos*), thus hinting, in its equestrian way, at his erstwhile penchant for long-distance travel (Germany, France, Spain), reminding us of Maugham's own wide travels which provided the diverse settings of his novels. But, more subtly, Philip's name harks back to that of another literary adventurer, one whose first name was regularly shortened to *Pip*, an expectant hero whose apprenticeship to Joe, the *black*smith, at the outset of that other, more famous semi-autobiographical novel, *Great Expectations*, very likely accounts in part for Maugham's abruptly shifting the name of the oyster locale of *Whit*stable to *Black*stable. (As a smith has his stable, so is black complementary to white.) It would appear that Dickens, too, was attracted to more than the white part of *Whit*stable, so to speak, that he went there for more than just the oysters, though his articles on the subject included "The Happy Fishing Grounds"[7] and "Another Whitstable Trade."[8] About a year later, in the same publication, he started *Great Expectations* in serial form. How Maugham conflated aspects of this novel along with *Copperfield* in his own quasi-autobiographical manner is the subject of another study.[9]

How much juice can be pressed out of a name? The central letters in *Philip* (*il*) point ahead to his life-long *ill*ness, as it were, his burdensome clubfoot, itself obviously based, as is well recognized, on Maugham's own physical deficiency—not a stutter (as often mislabeled), but a stammer. This subtlety should not be ignored, for Philip's limping walk constitutes a main basis for his bondage; he is obliged to try to overcome his awkward self-consciousness in feeling deformed and hence abnormally different. In *The Summing Up*, Maugham admitted that Philip's prayers to have the malformed foot cured paralleled his own similar early petitions concerning his vocal defect. When both supplications came to naught, the result was agnosticism. In itself, to make much of the *ill* sound in *Philip* may seem strained, were it not for the connotation also of a similar health problem in the surname, *Carey*, which hints at a deficiency like, say, a dental cavity. Thus the hero's becoming a physician to sacrifice himself for others assists as a vital compensation for, as well

Chapter XII: A Rose Window on Human Bondage

as displacement of, his private emotional tensions (harking back also to Maugham's own medical training).

In yet another complementary guise, Carey can be seen as an uncommonly sensitive young man, one given to much *caring*, if you will, in his conscientious way, but it is the *way* he cares that is of more critical interest. At times he thinks rather too much about his own plight; at others, he is unhappily obsessed in his yearning for the worthless Mildred. We think of Maugham's own life as well as the "portrait of the artist" in David Copperfield—Dickens again.

As if in deliberate counterpoint to the hero's full name, his uncle, the Vicar, has the assertive, formal first name of William (incidentally Maugham's own first), which can be assumed here to be a bit more than simply stock in its clearly reflecting on the prominent Victorian stress upon voluntarism, almost absurdly for its own sake at times, hence *willi*ng. (To transpose the first syllable metathetically to the end, William's name would duly stand for *Am I Will?* itself, a "palindrome" recalling Tennyson's stalwart credo: "To strive, to seek, to find, and not to yield.") The Victorians and their followers failed to recognize the extent to which the human will was motivated by factors outside its control, however, and thus were given to being *self*-willed, as is Uncle William.

Truly this William is a typically hard taskmaster, one all too stubbornly set in his avuncular insistence on having young Carey embrace the ministry and in resisting the nephew's adolescent, idealistic yearning to lead a sacrificial life as an artist; hence, for stern William, poor Philip tends to become one of (alas) those disrespectable bohemians. For models, Maugham had in mind, first of all, his own petulant uncle considered as posturing alongside three other assertive, paternalistic figures: the imposing Dr. Thomas Arnold (thus in *Bondage*, he cited Matthew Arnold, the more prominent son, along with some other Victorian notables), Ernest Pontifex's demanding sire in *The Way of All Flesh* (to which, it is known, Maugham owed a major general debt in *Bondage*), and, as a final exponent of sheer arduousness for its own sake, including a certain sadism, Dickens's forbidding Edward Murdstone, whose surname is the most chilling, but thereby befitting, of them all. The reader is expected to muse: "If only the Roman *Will* in *William* would combine with the Greek *Phileo* in *Philip*, thereby power with love...." The Edwardian divided self thus becomes a dark hallmark of the novel, yet a symbolic rose window lets in a little light, as we shall now see.

At the outset when little Philip heads so determinedly to school, a mandated courage so often during those arduous years, he happens to befriend a schoolmate known by his surname alone, as often was the English custom, a fellow with the name of *this* book's subject: Rose. In context, such a name by itself might, at first, seem overly floral for a male, especially for this extravert-athlete (Pete Rose notwithstanding)—the blushing flower being so frequently symbolic of primness and the sweetness of feminine pulchritude. But Maugham wanted to make certain that Carey's youthful heroworship for Rose was seen as clearly adumbrated from a literary point of view. How did he do that? He found it envisioned in the comparable camaraderie of David Copperfield and James Steerforth, even as the latter gave the younger classmate the condescending or playful nickname of *Daisy*. Whereas such a shortening of *David* may be thought of teasingly as a diminutive alone, it still was meant to reflect as well on the hero's innocence. For *Daisy* would connote the state of not having been deflowered.[10] If it was scarcely required for Maugham's Rose to have been, say, grafted off Dickens's Daisy, the onomastic correlation suggests at least a certain amount of similar cultivation. (We might contrast, in passing, the womanly figure of Rosie in *Cakes and Ale*).

Biographically, it might be urged, hints of Maugham's later admittedly deviate preferences could appear discernible already in Carey's boyish crush on Rose, for example in the former's abrupt recalcitrance shown in his taking on a new male companion named Sharp (whom Rose perfunctorily disdains), in retaliation for having been cut by Rose, the point being that to be cut by a Sharp/Rose combination can induce only bleeding, whereby we are apt to think, however obliquely, of Goethe again, his well-known poem "Heidenröslein." This reaction closely approximates what has often enough been popularly termed deviate "bitchiness," if you will. Is it then entirely coincidental that Philip's later obsession, the implacable Mildred, thinks of him as a trifle "queer" (475), by which she principally intends what is now so often meant by "invert" or "deviate"? At any rate, her usage might conceivably portend for him some comparable homoerotic inclinations. When he later declines to partake of full physical relations with her, she notably reiterates the denigrating epithet "queer." No doubt, his overt or normal

Chapter XII: A Rose Window on Human Bondage

rationalization for holding back could well derive from his natural suspicions as a physician: clinically, he could fear her having contracted a venereal disease, owing to her profession of streetwalker. True enough, in its English meaning, admittedly, the term "queer" in this context need not intimate inverted tendencies; yet it might include some, too, for Philip, after all, does disclose, in his typically introspective way, his feeling "not lucky with women" (371). This admission could point to his having other, hidden, plausibly even Maugham-like inclinations. Still, the more clear-cut issue is the significance for him of Mildred. So let us grapple with her ourselves on the onomastic level next.

Recent scholarship has revealed that, paradoxically, Mildred, the principal passion in Philip's life, was in point of fact based on a "youth" Maugham had once encountered.[11] The ordinary reader may well feel flabbergasted at such an unexpected disclosure. For do we not have some contradiction? Does it make good sense for "with-it" Mildred to put Philip down as "queer" for not making love to her and then to be herself based on a male model? But perhaps it does after all. One valid explanation is that Maugham was writing under the aegis of "the attraction of repulsion," a well-known Romantic shibboleth to which he was prone. Therefore, in one sense, Mildred was drawn to Philip even *because* of his seeming to be different (that is, courageously apart from the multitude). Yet in spite of Maugham's at least passing interest in the curious case of Oscar Wilde (also mentioned in *Bondage*), suspicion of sexual inversion in this context can be manifestly exaggerated. Presumably some hero-worship reveals itself in Philip's early fondness for Rose, but the issue of whether such attachment is proleptic of Maugham's own later preferences is, at best, ambiguous—Beverley Nichols's well-known biographical inferences in *A Case of Human Bondage*[12] and Ted Morgan's even more provocative recent disclosures[13] notwithstanding. Nichols, it might be cited in passing, does make the onomastic point of referring amusingly to the "-ham" in Maugham (36, 142), a connotation which may, in any event, have its serious side-effects in pointing to his thespian talents, both in public and private. (Thus compare also the connotation of *mummer* in *Maugham.*)

In turn, the name of Philip's other principal male friend, who plays a larger role in his later life, Hayward, is only slightly comparable to Rose's name in similarly hinting at a floral metaphor.

If not exactly the farmboy type, *Hayward* is still very much the dilettante. Analogously, Lawson, Carey's Parisian *confrère*, in being a "technically" competent enough artist, lives up to his own name by subscribing to the letter of the law of his trade, thereby being a "son" of such "Law," if not one especially gifted.

Less stock and hence more captivating is the surname of that incorrigible *poète maudit* Cronshaw, who is based on at least four familiar *décadents*: Oscar Wilde once again, Enoch Soames (Max Beerbohm's memorable dandy), the Canadian painter James Morria, and particularly the wicked Aleister Crowley. In Cronshaw's maverick character, all four are somehow conflated, although his notorious addiction to absinthe, as well as to sheer hedonism without moral stigma, most specifically conjures up Maugham's fascination with the perverse Satanism of Crowley. Might not then Cronshaw's very name derive somehow from Crowley's? If we indulge in a little name play, in a bewitching way it does: the first three letters in *Cronshaw* hark back to those in *Crowley* with the final letter rounding off the parallel by borrowing Crowley's fourth—almost as if in Satanic parody of the biblical Alpha and Omega. (As for the last three letters in *Crowley*, their effect can be taken as merely that of a diminutive appendage. This correlation again is strictly on the level of connotation, not etymology.) If we would hesitate before assigning such playful orthographic creativity to Maugham's conscious, at least we can point to his well-recognized deliberate use of Crowley in *The Magician* as unconsciously supportive. A little more magic than meets the eye may be involved.

As for Philip's own name as eliciting thoughts of love, as noted earlier, in a novel involving acute bondage to human relations heterosexual love naturally enough dominates. The extent of Carey's promiscuous attachments is inherent already in the name play, however subtly. His first relationship is with Emily Wilkinson, in deference to the onomastic precedent of Copperfield and his initial ardor for another "Em'ly."[14] True, one contrast of note is that Miss Wilkinson is considerably older than her paramour and is promiscuous with the hero, whereas "little Em'ly" runs off, not with the protagonist, but instead with the renegade Steerforth. But, in another valid sense, Wilkinson's very surname ingeniously anticipates her role: she is altogether amenable to the hero's youthful advances, thus "will kiss" (*Wil-ki-s*). Granted, such a reading may seem at first a bit *recherché*, but we must remember that what is

Chapter XII: A Rose Window on Human Bondage

involved is again valid connotation, not etymology. It might be added that if a lady too easily spells out what she will do, she can act rather indiscreetly. In any event, this Emily "will kiss" in deed. (Like William earlier, she has a strong will.)

At the end of Chapter XXXIII, the first buss is prominently enacted. Being adamant in wanting to prove to himself that he is manly, Carey allows her role to extend scarcely beyond that of common love-object. Thereafter, in Paris, while receiving her love letters in French, ones which gradually beset him, he runs into his second main female in his maturing world, the pathetic Fanny Price. Although again her name at first seems stock only, she can be tagged as a woeful soul who will indeed pay "-an[n]y price" for her desperate commitment to art and therewith to him. Having no aesthetic talent to speak of, she befriends the young hero, who accepts her love partly out of sheer embarrassment. Finally, she manages to do away with herself, her name thus parodying her unfortunate destiny. Such feminine types like Wilkinson and Price point to women in an imaginary Maugham world, one that he himself never made, paradoxically enough. At length we confront Norah, whose first name rhymes with another obviously Copperfieldian antecedent, thus obliquely recalling that of Dora, both young ladies playing the same role, that of an innocent creature in a complicated social milieu. Instead of a Dickensian "Dumb Dora," we have a "numb Norah," a bit of a drag.

Yet quite the most fascinating female counterpart is still Mildred Rogers, the *femme fatale* whose name may seem, on the surface, to be plain or representative only, thereby that of one who turns into a dull street-walker, as she does, her onomastic designation being pedestrian in more ways than one. One implicit connotation of her last name, however, is to copulate (to *roger*); another implication is its affirmative nature (*roger* as *yes*), again intimating her willingness to resign herself to street life. (Molly Bloom's yeses, her famous last words in *Ulysses*, reverberate.) Her rebel attitude, her theft of Philip's heart, along with her mercenary associations, make her out to be a female marauder type, thereby hoisting up for us the pirate insignia known as the Jolly *Roger*. Not to be forgotten is her being originally based on that "youth" Maugham once knew, her surname thus reflecting also the simple male name of Roger. As for other female names, the historically prior mystery of one Mary Rogers, a cigar-girl, who inspired Poe's Marie Rogêt, would also have a bearing. Because all these associations together add aplomb to what would otherwise seem to be a fairly uninspiring label, may they not play together, enriching her role onomastically? Dickens surely would not have disapproved.

As for her first name, more name play can be invoked. When Philip originally learns of *Mildred*, Maugham teases us about its seeming vulgarity. Carey's professed reaction is decidedly negative. "What an odious name," he tersely informs Dunford (268), whose own name does not seem to amount to much at first. Yet whereas he would dismiss it as "so pretentious," the latter admits to being rather taken by it. Why does Philip disapprove of it? Because of its formal, Victorian aura. Again we experience the "attraction of repulsion" at work. With its puritanical, organ-like tone, *Mildred* recalls the first syllable of *Mil*ton, or John Stuart *Mill*, both stalwarts having been adamant voluntarists—even as freedom from bondage is what is at issue in this otherwise Naturalistic, deterministic *Bildungsroman*. If hardly a direct throwback to England's leading Puritan poet in any cogent sense, Mildred may still ironically curtsey in the direction of Maugham's Romanticized or heretical reading of Milton's epic, if only because she is such a demonic soul. (Thus, *her* paradise is indeed lost.) Further, something in *Mil*dred might also convey both her, too, being *ill* and the French *mille* (meaning a thousand), implying the commercial element in her flagrant, whorish life style, as Pierre Horn reminds me.

In her first name, do we not also discern the effect of ungodly *dread*, the "echo" in her second relating to it by recalling for us the proverbial *mill*stone around the neck from the Bible? Hence "there was a *dread*ful humility in her bearing" (329), something like that of the "'umble Uriah Heep" in *Copperfield*, not to mention the likewise formidable Jane Murdstone. That is what indeed made Bette Davis so famous for her portrayal of this slattern in the film. Again, if Mildred was based at all on the "youth," then her first name, like her last, might be said to usher in a certain masculinity at least in its very formality, perhaps what Philip dreads. Again, whereas in real life such a convenient array of onomastic meanings is rather uncalled for, in art aesthetic principles are more operative and allowable, whereby connotations build up. The net effect is not really parodic but supportive.

In one specifically pretentious and ironic respect, Mildred is stubbornly Victorian: she strongly voices her objection to un-

Chapter XII: A Rose Window on Human Bondage 113

conventional display of nude pictures even when their officially *au naturel* purpose is clearly aesthetic, not concupiscent. This is an unexpected censure, we may feel, from an easy-going Nature girl or waitress-cum-prostitute. May she not, as Hamlet's mother had it, "protest too much"? True to form, she associates with a crude lover called Miller, the "naturalized German, who had Anglicized his name" (282). Maugham's awareness of political tensions between Britain and Germany leading to World War I doubtless was, in part, responsible. At any rate, the linguistic shift in Miller's assuming a new name hints at yet another coverup: she fails to realize in time that he is already married. Without doubt, the uncouth occupation of the miller type, already captured so memorably in Chaucer's leading ostentatious pilgrim, is inherent both in Mildred's lover's nature and in her onomastic relation with him. The first syllable of her name thereby "echoes" that of his last (*Mil-*), even as the second syllable of his own first name provides a textual "re-echo" (*E-mil*). The two, in a nominal sense, were made for each other. Further, Em*il Mil*ler doubly suggests his being *ill*-suited. A subtle enough craftsman, Maugham was not beyond such subliminal onomastic effects, however subtextual.

After being forsaken by Miller, she is taken up by Griffiths, whose surname likewise links with hers in conjuring up the demonic and predatory in its strange, animalistic link with the clawed griffin; then she has a short-lived relationship with him, as might be expected, in that this griffin takes wing and leaves. In itself, this onomastic matter may at first seem trivial, but the incident is worth some biographical pause because of its incidental effect upon the Naturalist Dreiser, who was largely responsible for inaugurating the novel's immense American popularity, having written the enthusiastic Preface for its first edition here after it was not well received in Europe. Although he claimed that he was mainly indebted to the Chester Gillette case when he composed his best-known work, he casually transformed the name to *Clyde Griffiths*, preserving the original influence and initials but adding, in turn, a resonance of Maugham's *Griffiths*. For in both novels the Griffiths name designates the smart type who rejects a young woman with whom he has had an affair, thereby designating the bounder and acting the part of the mythic griffin, whose wings symbolize its wish to escape. In transferring his Griffiths from Maugham's, however, Dreiser switched from a pathetic to a tragic life situation, thereby giving by implication his initial source of *literary* inspiration richer resonance.

Other names in *Bondage* are not so striking, but the vital ones stand out, and some comparison may be possible with other Maugham novels. Aside from the confessional use of the name *Willie*, little onomastic interest seems extant in his *Cakes and Ale*, yet such a verdict as "beauty is a bit of a bore"[15] perhaps hints again at "the attraction of repulsion." Again Dickensian influence is self-evident (82, 125, 144), and Goethe is cited once more (29), though the main debt may be to Hardy's *Tess of the d'Urbervilles*.[16] Reverting to *Bondage*, we can sense more gravitation of polar contraries, so to speak, in such love-entanglements as that of a Chinese with a German, a minor meeting of East and West. Philip's being enamored with Emily also reveals such magnetic attachment as exhibited in his finding her repulsive just before making love to her:

> She looked grotesque. Philip's heart sank as he stared at her; she had never seemed so unattractive; but it was too late now. (149)

Why? Because he felt compelled to assert his manliness regardless. Martin Seymour-Smith has conjectured that Maugham was attempting here to resolve "some of the problems of his own ambisexuality,"[17] yet Maugham himself would have been disinclined to take such depth psychology very seriously (although perhaps thereby underrating, in effect, his own creativity). As Ivor Brown tells us, "He had long turned against the High Froth of a recondite vocabulary and was not impressed by the even more turbid foam of Depth Psychology."[18] In any event, Em*ily* links with Em*il* as *ill*-suited rejects.

In an overriding final sense, Carey typifies man's human condition, his being riven by physical desires which conflict with his spiritual, aesthetic ideals. Philip therefore has it coming to him: after dismissing two women who sincerely cared for him, Emily and Fanny, he has to take the consequences when the woman he thinks he does want cruelly reviles him. His final conquest then, Sally Athelny, turns out to be companionable enough, but aesthetically she is a nonentity like Norah, thus in stark contrast to the bold reality of Mildred. As an "Agnes figure" evidently deriving again from *Copperfield*, she reveals her nondescript character in the flatness of her name. Sally's neat stability is analogous to Agnes Wickfield's, yet such healthy stasis produces a more or less humdrum character. Michael Slater, an authority on Dickens's women, is notably critical of Agnes,[19] and Maugham, in turn, admitted that readers had found the ending of his novel the least satisfactory part. At best, Sally is the one for whom Philip, as would-be dashing knight in shining armor, would make a "sally," even if no real tournament is in the making. In striking contrast, Mildred's actually resonant name hints at more complexity through Maugham's ironic adaptation of typically English understatement.

In short, the import of *Bondage* resides hardly in its mere realistic, sometimes low-keyed depiction of the commonplaces of modern life, but it does in the heightened effect produced by the characters interacting onomastically among themselves. Helpfully serving as thematic bonds, the leading names provide signposts, ones which, if not as theatrically imaginative as some of Dickens's, in any case with Philip and Sally point to an optimistically human destination, not to some *cul-de-sac*. We can hope. If then life is not to be scanned always through rose-colored glasses here, some light and thereby enlightenment can still filter in metaphorically through what we can call Maugham's rose window. Biographical highlights partly point the way to our unveiling these onomastic effects, in keeping with Maugham's stated preferences and his comments on Dickens's own "autobiographical" fiction, but they do not in themselves psychologically tell the whole tale—even as Art, in general, functions on a different level from Life. Nonetheless, the use of clever naming procedures, however subtle, can prove to be a critical desideratum.

Notes

1. References are to *Of Human Bondage*, introd. Somerset Maugham (Harmondsworth: Penguin, 1972).

2. Cited by John Bennett Shaw in his "Afterword" to Arthur Conan Doyle's *The Doings of Raffles Haw* (Bloomington: Gaslight Publications, 1981), p. 147.

3. From Conan Doyle's 1921 talk as duplicated in part by Donald A. Redmond in *Sherlock Holmes: A Study in Sources* (Kingston: McGill-

Queen's University Press, 1982), p. 303. (With *Tittletits*, he evidently meant *Tappertits*, which he humorously conflated with *Tittlebats*.)

4. New York: Doubleday, Doran, 1940, p. 39.

5. See R. F. Fleissner, "Of Dickensian Bondage: A Probe," *Research Studies* (Washington State University), 48 (1980), 50–56.

6. The biographer, Ted Morgan, is cited that way by Forrest D. Burt, in *W. Somerset Maugham* (Boston: Twayne, 1985), p. 15.

7. *All the Year Round*, 26 November 1859.

8. Ibid., 14 January 1860.

9. See n. 5 above.

10. Pamela Hansford Johnson, in "The Sexual Life in Dickens's Novels," in *Dickens 1970: Centenary Essays*, ed. Michael Slater (London: Chapman and Hall, 1970), pp. 173–94, observed, in writing of Steerforth and David, that "the latter is nicknamed Daisy" (p. 180), but without drawing any conclusions from this odd sobriquet for a young man.

11. See J. Dobrinsky, *La Jeunesse de Somerset Maugham* (Paris: Didier, 1976), p. 105. He also details more of Maugham's debt to Dickens. (Burt, pp. 65–66, sees a basis for Mildred in Sue Jones.)

12. London: Secker and Warburg, 1966.

13. New York: Simon and Schuster, 1979.

14. In my previous study (see n. 5 above), I did not consider the ostensible ramifications of the names of Emily, Norah, Sally, et al., but confined myself largely to the Mildred/Estella comparison in terms of the *femme fatale* type.

15. Penguin ed., p. 97.

16. Burt, p. 150.

17. *Who's Who in Twentieth Century Literature* (New York: McGraw Hill, 1977), p. 233.

18. *W. Somerset Maugham* (Cranbury, N.J.: A. S. Barnes, 1970), p. 26.

19. *Dickens and Women* (Stanford: Stanford University Press, 1983), pp. 250–51 et passim.

Part IV

Roses and Special Effects

"Rose, O reiner Widerspruch"
—Rilke

This last grouping represents a miscellaneous section which includes pieces not easily fitting under another rubric, yet it is meant as something more than an addendum. Although somewhat more specialized, these three chapters are concerned with prime factual considerations, as in the precise textual reading of one of literature's best known and loved rose poems, the exact meaning and source of not only *The Name of the Rose* but its own name; finally, a highly condensed summary of events at a fairly recent, extremely well-received rose conference helps to round the book out, providing a *raison d'être* for this study: its "popular culture" appeal.

Constable's most famous sonnet, "My Lady's Presence," undoubtedly was one of the world's leading rose poems but has thus far not received due scholarly attention; among other connections, it ties in with Shakespeare again, as in Chapter I, and the question of number lore involved in it provides a cross-reference to the chapters on Frost. Umberto Eco's work has already resulted in a number of scholarly volumes based on it; its clear use of the Sherlock Holmes tradition harks back to Chapter III, whereas its medieval scope ties in with Constable's Catholic tradition. Eco's express statement that he meant his rose symbol ambiguously can be challenged, thus having us delve more deeply into the subliminal symbolism behind his title and the way it is then reflected in the text. The final chapter also bears on Eco and his bestseller, the main focus at the rose conference, which, however, embraced many roseate areas and thus may itself be called multi-petaled. It transcended the usual sort of local conference displaying immediate talent in a given area and thus may convey some universal import to the reader, the chief speakers, for example, having international reputations and various papers appearing in nationally known journals afterwards. It is hoped that the success of this conference, with its Eco session as climactic, may inspire others in the future somehow related to it. At least rose societies are still in abundance, and floral interests never seem to die out, unlike the botanical member itself.

Thus ends this literary rose-garland. The final test is if the reader can pluck his own rose therefrom and make it aesthetically meaningful in his own way. Anagogically speaking, the purpose of much of this section and book will have then been fulfilled—*toto caelo*. If everything will finally be coming up roses, we would have *une vie en rose* indeed—a goal to be sought, if not always attainable in real life (as opposed to the world of art).

Chapter XIII

Henry Constable's "My Lady's Presence Makes the Roses Red": A Reappraisal

The Poem Itself

I. The original 1592 version[1]

My Ladies presence makes the Roses red,
  because to see her lips, they blush for shame:
  the Lillies leaves (for envie) pale became,
  and her white hands in them this envie bred:
The Marigold the leaves abroad doth spred,
  because the sunnes: and her power is the same:
  the Violet of purple colour came,
  di'd in the bloud she made my hart to shed.
In briefe, all flowers from her their vertue take;
  from her sweete breath, their sweet smells doo proceed,
  the living heate which her eie beames doth make,
  warmeth the ground, and quickeneth the seed:
    The raine wherewith she watereth the flowers,
    falls from mine eyes, which she dissolves in
        showers.

II. A recent revised version[2]

My Ladies presence makes the roses red
Because to see her lips they blush for shame
The lilies leaues for envy pale became
And her white hands in them this envy bred

> The marygold abroad the leaues did spread
> Because the suns and her power is the same
> The violet of purple coloure came
> Dy'd withe the bloud she made my heart to shed
>
> In briefe all flowers from her theyre vertue take
> From her sweet breath theyre sweet smells doe proceed
> The liuing heate which her eybeames doe make
> Warmeth the ground and quickneth the seede
> > The rayne wherewith she watereth these flowers
> > Falls from myne eyes which she dissolues in shewers.

Because Constable's most typical sonnet, which will be henceforth identified as "My Lady's Presence," is probably the best known nowadays (quoted, for example, in a standard college text, the *Norton Introduction to Literature*, which boasts also a notable gathering of rose poems to enliven the student),[3] and because of my new edition of his 1592 *Diana*,[4] it is fitting to indulge in some comment on this presumably model sonnet, one which then also constitutes a hallmark in the history of classic rose literature. How *model* the sonnet is, is a question, however, because some would argue that it presents stereotypical poetic conventions of the time more than it has real, intrinsic, aesthetic merit. Indeed, the Norton editors saw fit to include it only along with Shakespeare's familiar no. 130 ("My Mistress' Eyes Are Nothing Like the Sun"), which can be easily taken, and has often been, as a parody of such fashion, possibly even satiric of "My Lady's Presence" in particular, for a number of parallels (including the rose image) also appear there.

In brief, the Constable sonnet figures as no. 17 in the 1592 *Diana* sequence, which was advisedly used as the base text for the recent edition, one which amounted to an editing of the earliest edition, hence providing evidence of original intent. (This approach had been sanctioned for me some years ago already by Ruth Hughey of Ohio State University.) Its textual problems happen to be relatively sparse compared with those in other sonnets in the gathering. One discrepancy is that whereas the new edition sees the first line of the couplet as "The raine wherewith she watereth *the* flowers," Evans[5] and Grundy prefer the more localized reading, namely "*these* flowers," which is found in the so-called Dyce MS. The authority of that manuscript, however, is open to some question, if

Chapter XIII: Constable's "My Lady's Presence..."

only because of its vast number of variant readings, some of which are extremely extensive. In spite of its inclusion of what is called Constable's recantation for writing secular poetry, it is clearly possible, even likely, that Dyce represents a copy worked over by another hand, thus misleadingly providing alternative versions of what he wrote. Hence Sir Sidney Lee wrote that "[t]he Sonnets of ... Constable long circulated in manuscript, and suffered much the same fate as Shakespeare's at the hands of piratical publishers";[6] further, Ruth Hughey, in transcribing the version of the *Diana* from the Arundel Harington manuscript of Tudor poetry for the first time, indicated in no uncertain terms that the Dyce variations "must surely be contrary to the author's meaning" and went so far as to announce that she could see "no reason why the independent variants in C [namely, Dyce] need serious consideration."[7] On the other hand, because the Grundy edition, which is widely and uncritically accepted now as standard, relies so heavily on Dyce (notably in such a key passage as the fourth line in such a well-known sonnet as "Blame Not My Heart"), it is in definite need of reappraisal. Fortunately, in the case of "My Lady's Presence," variants are few, making the textual issue less complex.

In any event, Constable had left England early in the last decade of the sixteenth century, owing largely to his conversion to Roman Catholicism, the old faith he could not legally practice in his native country; so it is difficult to imagine that he himself would have been responsible for all or even most of the later variant readings, whether they be aesthetically preferable or not at times. It is a commonplace that, as the editors of Shakespeare's First Folio tell us, "diverse stolne, and surreptitious copies, maimed, and deformed by the frauds and stealthes of injurious imposters"[8] were widely circulating, a major reason for the editors' settling on a "final" text of the plays. (True, nowadays their acumen has again been put to the test by the New Revisionists.) Consequently, it stands to good reason that a diplomatic text of Constable's poetry is also worth preserving, as in the first version, here presented.

As for the contrast with Shakespeare's sonnets in general, a comparison with Shakespeare's flower poetry, for example, not merely the apparently obvious satire in no. 130, is worth serious consideration. Already in 1872, Massey saw in "My Lady's Presence" quite reasonably "one of the few possible sources of a Shakespeare sonnet."[9] Further, "the opening conceit of Constable's sonnet," wrote a recent comparatist, Gerald Hammond, "is more immediately attractive than anything in Shakespeare's sonnet,"[10] by which he meant no. 99, which is also compared with Constable's in the new edition.[11] Then Joan Grundy pointed out how both poets in these respective poems made use of almost the same flowers, if prettily enough in a different arrangement: "Constable mentions the rose, lily, marigold, and violet; Shakespeare the violet, lily, marjoram, and rose."[12] Was it not characteristic of Shakespeare to bring in an herb because of his great natural, domestic attraction to simples, as found so frequently throughout his plays, scarcely only in *Romeo and Juliet* (for which see Chapter I)?

More captivating yet, both Constable's and Shakespeare's flowers take on human qualities: "Constable's roses blush for shame; so do Shakespeare's," she said. Whereas overall comparisons like these can be often recognized as "commonplace in themselves or a natural development of other commonplaces," Miss Grundy rightly inferred that "their numerical strength ... makes a borrowing on Shakespeare's part seem likely." She offered a decent, subtle piece of evidence for such a correlation: in the preceding sonnet by the Stratford poet we hear this of the flowers:

> They we[a]re but sweet, but figures of delight:
> Drawne after you, you patterne of all those.

Consider:*Drawne after you*. Could the "upstart Crow" not have had the *Diana* in the back of his mind with these lines? Grundy at least saw a *hidden* allusion to Constable, concluding that "the fact that in other sonnets [Shakespeare] mocked at these fashions does not invalidate the conclusion that Constable was regarded as one of their leading exponents." Nor does it invalidate by implication the likelihood that Shakespeare did not always parody but sometimes liked simply to follow in the train of fashion.

Wisely Grundy preferred not to employ the controversial historicist word *influence* with regard to the Shakespeare-Constable correlation, finding such a commitment "rather too strong." True, she was hardly being merely coy or oversubtle in this matter, for it *is* very difficult to prove absolute indebtedness in such cases. Ironically, the same sensitive point, the difficulty of accommodating *influence* as a viable term, was made independently by the reviewer of Grundy's book for the London *Times Literary Supplement*, again with regard to Shakespeare, as criticism of her work presumably, whereas, in point

Chapter XIII: Constable's "My Lady's Presence..."

of fact, this demurrer was only corroborating what she herself had already acknowledged openly.

Another poet who, incidentally, also borrowed from "My Lady's Presence" most probably in Shakespeare's time (although, again, this cannot be definitely proved), was Sir William Alexander; his key line, noted by Grundy, was "The Roses did the rosie hue envy...."[13] She then added: "The popularity of this sonnet, with others beside Shakespeare, is considerable," inspiring, among the contemporaries, Daniel, Drayton, Barnes, and Barnfield.

With regard to the text of "My Lady's Presence" again, one apparently syntactic problem is Constable's use of *doth* in l. 11 ("the living heate which her eie beames *doth* make"). Here the Dyce and Harington MSS provide the reading *do*, presumably meant as a *corrigendum*, one which seems grammatically superior, especially in terms of the proper agreement between subject and verb in the immediately preceding line. (Both the *Oxford English Dictionary* and Abbott's *Shakespearian Grammar* reveal no evidence that the rules for agreement were any different then or that *doth* was permissible at times in place of *do*.) In the new edition, it is concluded that because "subject-verb agreement was sometimes rather loosely adhered to in the Renaissance, it is unnecessary to emend the text in an old-spelling edition."[14] That statement need not be emended now, if only because flagrant errors in such syntax did occur, more so perhaps than today among the *literati*; moreover, a similar problem emerges in the sonnet "Faire By Inheritance." True enough, the eleventh line in "My Lady's Presence," as found in the 1592 edition, could give the ludicrous impression that heat is what makes the lady's eye beams. What the poet clearly meant, though, is only that the heat of the loving eyes metaphorically warms the heart.

Yet we have some basis for retaining the original word even if it is, by the standards of modern grammatical niceties, a bit misleading. First of all, aside from the general, well-known commonplace that grammar, notably spelling, was not standardized then as it is today, poetic license cannot be so lightly disregarded. In this instance, the poet could well have initially preferred the phrase "doth make" to "do make" precisely because the latter would jingle-jangle with "do proceed" in the line just preceding. We have plenty of examples of such poetic attempts to avoid repetition (as well as of faulty readings resulting from careless scribal repetitions). Moreover, numerous awkwardnesses do occur in Shakespeare's own texts, whereupon scholars still retain the old-spelling and old-syntax versions; often the punctuation is altered, but that was in some cases the compositor's, as may also be the case with Constable.[15] (Admittedly there are times when the meter in a Shakespearean line would suggest not only the proper spelling or form of a word, but whether or not the *right* word is in evidence. This is the case, for example, with the familiar "Indian"/"Iudean" crux in *Othello*, 5.2.347.) Further, clumsiness in syntax or word choice hardly interferes in our recollections of some of the most popular of Renaissance texts. To take a well-known example, the Lord's Prayer in the KJV reads "Our Father *which* art in heaven," yet who would want to replace the relative pronoun with the more accurate *who*? Finally, it is arresting that the controversial form *doth* appeared as well in the *second* edition of the *Diana* (1594), one which did correct some of the more obvious *errata* in the first. So quite conceivably the printer simply did not consider *doth* an *erratum*. (Should the non-specialist reader find all this to-do over such a minor textual reading hopelessly pedantic, all we can say is that he may be quite right. The best answer is the truism that conservative textual scholarship may just as readily take such an "indictment" as basically a compliment.)

As for another variant reading, "di'd *in* the bloud" (dyed in the blood), in line eight, seems rather more idiomatic than "Dy'd *with* the bloud" as the Dyce, Harington, and Grundy versions have it, even though the ninth line clumsily starts off with the same preposition ("In"). It might be contended that to *die in* something suggests a form of death, obviously a pun not intended, more than *die with*, but such a scruple appears uncalled for, especially when at times the notion of dying in the sense of expiring was occasionally associated with release of sperm. At least it was often a bit later, in the seventeenth century, with John Donne and the Metaphysicals, but there were probably some forerunners too. The stronger case for *die in*, as opposed to *die with*, is surely that the former is more natural in the spoken language, and the prim naturalness of Constable's poetry is one of its chief attractions, in spite of his liking to play little tricks with the old conceits as well.[16]

The title for "My Lady's Presence" given in the Grundy edition is absent from the 1592 edition, contains numerological implications, and appears in general rather *too* flowery (that is, in the wrong sense): "The thyrd 7 of seuerall occasions and accidents / happening in the life tyme of his loue / Of his Mistresse vpon

Chapter XIII: Constable's "My Lady's Presence..." 127

occasion of her walking in a garden."[17] Affirming that this title was Constable's own later revision appears to be rather conjectural. The clear-cut simplicity of his poetry does not easily invite the intrusion of number lore here, although a later sonnet does deal with the number seven in the commonplace example of summing up the Seven Deadly Sins. How do we cope then with such an occult concern, if that is what it is?

Because of the vogue for numerology in the Renaissance and its use in some of the sonnet sequences, we should not definitely rule out its possible presence also with Constable, but so far sufficient proof seems lacking. The "thyrd 7" here is but one example of numerological designations later applied throughout the *Diana* by some scribe. Constable's conversion to Catholicism is neither here nor there, Protestant poets like Spenser also having followed the Neo-Pythagorean tradition at times. It could be claimed that if Shakespeare was borrowing from Constable, and he himself indulged in number lore in his sonnets, then he was inspired by that in the *Diana*, but such a hypothesis is hard to entertain with good supportive evidence. (On the other hand, because Robert Frost's poetry can be somewhat related to number lore, as in Chapter X, this possible accommodation should certainly not be ruled out in the works of a poet written when such esoteric symbolism was in its heyday.)

At any rate, in a similar manner it could be suggested that the enigmatic printer's note in the 1594 edition of the *Diana*, with its veiled allusiveness (glancing at Constable's perhaps controversial political position apropos of Turnus and Aeneas), looks ahead to the same kind of veiled allusion found in the dedication to Shakespeare's *Sonnets* (e.g., "Obscur'd wonders"), but again such an abstruse parallel represents a rather long shot. On the other hand, both Constable and Shakespeare are notably *sweet* in their creativity: whereas the former was known even as "England's sweet nightingale," one of his sonnets commencing "Sweet hand the sweet,"[18] the greater genius wrote his so-called "sugred" sonnets and then was called "sweetest Shakespeare" (Milton's "L'Allegro"). In sum, we can hardly help contrasting the Constable lines in "My Lady's Presence" and those in Shakespeare's ninety-ninth sonnet with the familiar Valentine's Day jingle: "Roses are red, violets are blue, / Sugar is sweet, and so are you." Just because these lines have become such a bromide in today's world, it is now profitable to return to the early poets who gave the words their truer, inherent meaning. Hence this essay.

In general, although Grundy's edition is eclectic and too much indebted to the Dyce MS, her scholarship in general is quite accurate and most of her comments commendatory. (She does miss one variant in her collations for "My Lady's Presence": in line 6, the word *power* is spelled as *powr* in the Harington MS—only a minor spelling variant that she fails to cite. Still, the total number of such omissions in the sonnets as a whole would eventually have to be taken into account.) The orthography she uses, if not entirely in accord with the first old-spelling edition and sometimes at odds with the meter (for instance, her use of "quickneth" rather than "quickeneth" in l. 12, which may be a typo), at least preserves much of the flavor of the lines and makes for ease in modern reading, if at times it also seems affected. These points are important with regard to "My Lady's Presence" if we want every petal of that rose precise. For this is a lyric which, as M. M. Reese has put it, expresses the lover's sense of desolation "in modish conceits about the beloved's cruelty,"[19] thus being a perfect specimen of its time. A typical, memorable instance of such a conceit is one to end on here:

> The Violet of purple colour came,
> di'd in the bloud she made my hart to shed.

Notes

1. Transcribed in my edition, *Resolved to Love: The 1592 Edition of Henry Constable's "Diana" Critically Considered* (Salzburg: University of Salzburg, 1980), p. 19. (I use modern "v.")

2. From *The Poems of Henry Constable*, ed. Joan Grundy (Liverpool: Liverpool University Press, 1960), p. 130. See also *Elizabethan Sonnets*, ed. Maurice Evans (London: Dent, 1977), which also reprints the 1592 edition but emends it and does not include all the poems.

3. 3rd ed., ed. Carl E. Bain et al. (New York: Norton, 1981), pp. 663–68.

4. See n. 1 above.

5. Evans, p. 160.

6. *A Life of William Shakespeare* (New York: MacMillan, 1912), p. 92.

7. *The Arundel Harington Manuscript of Tudor Poetry*, 2 vols. (Columbus: Ohio State University Press, 1960) as indicated in the Appendix to my edition, p. 88.

8. Transcribed from the Norton Facsimile of the Folio of 1623, ed. Charlton Hinman (New York: W. W. Norton, 1968).

9. Cited by Gerald Hammond, *The Reader and Shakespeare's Young Man Sonnets* (Totowa: Barnes and Noble, 1981), p. 146.

10. Hammond, loc. cit.

11. *Resolved to Love*, p. 68.

12. Grundy, p. 61.

13. Grundy, p. 63.

14. *Resolved to Love*, p. 68.

15. "And a few clumsy phrases apart, the grammatical structure of the sonnets is so firm that those in the Todd MS. may be read quite easily, even though they are almost entirely unpunctuated" (Grundy, p. 73). This could imply that Constable was not responsible for the punctuation in the 1592 edition either, a matter left up to the printer or compositor.

16. "His diction is ... his greatest single asset, and for one quality in particular, its naturalness" (Grundy, p. 73).

17. Grundy, p. 130.

18. Notice also that the subtitle of the *Diana* was *The Praises of his Mistres in certaine sweete Sonnets.*

19. *Shakespeare: His World and His Work*, rev. ed. (New York: St. Martin's Press, 1980), p. 288.

Chapter XIV

Die Rose ist ohne Warum?
The Name of *The Name of the Rose*

Exactly whence did the title of Umberto Eco's celebrated novel derive? In his *Postscript* to it,[1] he indicated from Bernard de Morlay, a twelfth-century Benedictine, who was the source of the allusion in the novel's last line ("stat rosa pristina nomine, nomina nuda tenemus"),[2] yet he also clearly revealed what he said was his intended ambiguity in this respect. In a word, a title which is normally expected to be explanatory was meant, in this case, to be paradoxically the opposite, to be more interesting that way. In this chapter, let us relieve the reader's anxiety about this apparent affront to his intellect by suggesting that, after all is said and done, this title *does* have its meaning. Otherwise, we would have to take the role of the Rev. Andrew Greeley, the noted author of detective fiction, who made fun of what Eco did (if only, incidentally, to promote the mysteries of Ellis Peters instead): "Unlike Umberto Eco, she does not believe that the purpose of the title of a story is to confuse the reader...."[3] He goes on to make the curious statement that although "Eco undoubtedly describes truth" and "Peters, for her part, has only verisimilitude," the latter "makes for a better story than truth" (238). But not so, Reverend Father, if Christ is the Truth? In any case, it might be urged that such a flat view suggests a naïve understanding of the significance of literary "ambiguity," its levels of meaning.

Let us begin by glossing the quotation from Bernard de Morlay as follows: a dead thing, like an ancient rose, can be considered to exist—only because of its name. What does, then, a dead, ancient *rose* suggest?

One answer can be found implicitly also in the work of another modern fiction writer, William Faulkner. In a recent comment on his tale "A Rose for Emily," it was suggested that the title alludes to pressing "a rose between the pages of some seldom used book, to dry and preserve the token."[4] Miss Emily would know the value of such a token, for she writes on "note paper of an archaic shape" and in "faded ink." This can be a "proof that love once flourished, as looking at and holding that preserved rose are ways to revive precious memories. . . ." But then the rose in the book is merely a *symbol* of the past—in effect like Eco's rose title.

As in Faulkner, Eco's primary symbolism behind the rose is probably love, as also with Dante's mystic rose and thereby Christ and Mary as medieval roses. As expected, Eco cites Dante *en passant* in his *Postscript*, but we need also to recollect the love affair that boldly flourishes in the precise center of his novel—hence perhaps indebted to Dante, too, his figure of Love in the *Vita Nuova*, if only ironically—but also more explicitly to *The Song of Songs* in terms of the rich, biblical vocabulary used. Because of the import of the biblical book in literary terms, evidently the novelist was indebted to yet another Bernard than the one he mentioned. If so, it would be to one who put great emphasis upon the import of Solomon's Song, namely Bernard de Clairvaux.[5] Thus it has been said that not even "John of the Cross has contributed more lavishly to literature of *The Song of Songs* than Bernard of Clairvaux."[6] He composed eighty-six homilies and two commentaries on only the first two chapters. Although the application of the biblical book to Eco's novel is for the sake of one erotic episode, the extensive reference to diabolic temptation in this context compensates for any otherwise too secular a setting.

Yet in spite of these associations, critics have argued semiotically that the title reveals "the lack of a real correspondence between name (symbol) and thing (rose)."[7] In this regard, Eco denied the apparently common assumption that his label directly owed something to Juliet's query about what is in a name, saying that "it seems to me that the sense of Juliet's words is exactly the opposite of that of Bernard's. She suggests that names do not matter and do not affect the substance of the thing-in-itself."[8] (His last term, latently, hints at his accepting a Neo-Kantian philosophic stance.) Yet was not

Chapter XIV: Die Rose ist ohne Warum?

Eco inadvertently conflating Juliet's intent with Shakespeare's? The point surely is that although *she* sees nothing in a mere label, the names *do* play a vital role in this drama (as they have in this book); if it were not for the enmity between the families named Capulet and Montague, this tragedy would not be taking place. Consequently the net effect of her line is ironic; likewise that of Eco's title may be, for it can tell us something while hinting at almost nothing. Both play and novel are roses by another name. (So also the Rose Theatre.)

Might the confusion as to the meaning of the title link with the key controversy over whether monastic laughter is finally permissible? Should the title be considered at all as humorous misdirection, it would put Eco on the side of his anti-detective, William, who allowed for comedy even in religion. This suggestion is appealing, in some ways, because the idea that humor is good for the soul—is "*to make truth laugh,*" as William puts it[9]—is not only humanistic in the best Terentian sense but has some divine sanction. After all, even the Good Book itself quotes Jehovah as saying "Ha, ha," and then there is the commonplace that the Church was founded on a pun (albeit an uncomic one). Recently it has been shown that wordplay in the New Testament is subtle because it demands considerable knowledge of the Old, paronomasia being based on the interconnection.

But then some reviewers would rather laugh *at* than *with* Eco. The *Time* reviewer,[10] for example, after carefully noting that Eco used his title as a reflection of the Middle Ages on the infinite power of words, concluded somewhat indelicately, "*res, non verba*" (more substance, please, fewer words). Admittedly, some of the novel is hard for the layman to get through because of its untranslated Latin. Now a convenient handbook to help him has been made available.[11] On the other hand, Richard Ellmann, in his review, did not hesitate to speak of Eco's "delightful humor."[12] The reviewer for *America* found the novel treating "a number of red herrings,"[13] so we might ask whether the title may be one too. But is it?

In response, let us visualize the tripartite structure the last reviewer saw in the novel as actually corroborating the rose theme of the title, if indirectly: (1) The waning of the Middle Ages (thus only the name of the rose, not its real, mystical significance, seems important), (2) humor in Christian life (thus alluding to humor also in the title in the teasing interplay between name and referent), and

(3) Adso's coming of age (thus the rose finally gets ready to bloom, though it is still only nominal).

Another titular meaning worth considering is related more specifically to Eco's well-known semiotic interests. Franco Ferruci, in one of the more favorable reviews,[14] showed that although William always has something to instruct Adso, Eco elsewhere indicates that for the reality of death there is no semiotic interpretation. In a word, relativism or subjectivity has to have its limits. Ferruci indicates that this might mean that the rose of the title is unchanging, too, eternal like death, but that other things have to change all the time. This view is heading in the right direction. A further gloss would be Eco's in his introduction to a compilation of scholarly articles on his work called *Naming the Rose*, wherein he claimed that he was not consciously putting his semiotic principles into practice in writing the novel. (He did, however, refer to them in declining to evaluate what scholars had said about him.)[15]

Finally, two points may still be made about his rose symbolism apropos of modern literary criticism. First, Stein's familiar rose line (see Chapter VIII) reverts to mind, and Eco does cite it, among others, in his *Postscript* (3). The seeming tautology of her line, when viewed narrowly, may suggest that all that is involved is the repetition of the word "rose"—hence the "name of the rose" would exist in that sense as well. Yet, in point of fact, Stein was really referring to a woman, though Eco may not have been aware of that. At any rate, the question of how apropos the Stein allusion is, except in terms of surface appeal, is ultimately debatable.

Another point apropos of modern criticism is that Jacques Derrida has had a good bit to say on rose symbolism in relation to his favorite subject, Deconstructionism, a topic which clearly ties in with Eco's semiotic vision. For example, he has shown how a famous line of a dying woman—"Quick, a perfect rose"—has its peculiar poignancy, although what really comes across is again merely the "name" of that rose: "a perfect rose."[16]

Is there some mystical meaning in Eco's title? He was ambiguous on this point (and has been associated, for what it may be worth, with Leftist politics), but insofar as the rose's link to love, as formerly in *Le Roman de la Rose*, makes somewhat ambiguous the extent to which it revealed courtly love as influencing mystical love (or vice versa), so the amatory goings-on in Eco's house of God have a certain kind of precedent. Finally, the anachronism of having a

Chapter XIV: Die Rose ist ohne Warum?

Sherlockian figure, William of Baskerville, set to solve the mystery, but finding that it has really been solving him, so to speak, may have a precedent as well in Eco's awareness that Stein reinterpreted mystical rose symbolism, derived ultimately mainly from Dante (as her coterie friendship with Eliot would suggest), in her own way, whereby her famous four roses can be seen as constituting a perfect symmetrical circle:

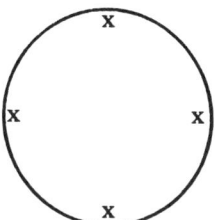

We might compare the well-known influence of cubism upon her writing, as if, in Dantean fashion, squaring the circle.

Further rose symbolism and mysticism somewhat relevant to Eco were evident in the Rev. Théodore Koehler's paper presented in the rose conference to be discussed next. His paper appeared afterwards in several publications, including the newspaper at the University of Dayton (where he manages the Marian Library) and *Our Lady's Digest*. Regrettably, he was unable to stay to comment on Eco's rose in the session following his, but perhaps (like the Rev. Greeley) he was put off by the deviant goings-on of *Il Nome della Rosa*. *De gustibus*. . . .

Notes

1. *Postscript to "The Name of the Rose,"* trans. William Weaver (New York: Harcourt Brace, 1983), p. 1.

2. References are to the softcover edition (New York: Warner Books, 1984); the final, "explanatory" line is on p. 611.

3. "Ellis Peters: Another Umberto Eco," *The Armchair Detective*, 18 (1985), 238.

4. Elizabeth Carney Kurtz, "Faulkner's 'A Rose for Emily,'" *The Explicator*, 44 (1986), 40.

5. See my note, "Adso's Closing Line in *The Name of the Rose Again*," *ANQ* (University of Kentucky), 2 (1989), 20–21.

6. See Linda Van Norden, *The Black Feet of the Peacock: The Color-Concept 'Black' from the Greeks Through the Renaissance* (Lanham, Maryland: University Press of America, 1985), p. 57.

7. See Stefano Tani, p. 71.

8. *Postscript*, p. 83.

9. *The Name of the Rose*, p. 598.

10. *Time*, 13 June 1983, p. 72.

11. Adele J. Haft et al., *The Key to the Name of the Rose* (Harrington Park, N.J.: Ampersand Associates, 1987).

12. *New York Review of Books*, 21 July 1983, p. 11.

13. *America*, 13 August 1983, pp. 75–76.

14. *New York Times Book Review*, 5 June 1983, pp. 1ff.

15. Umberto Eco, "Prelude to a Palimpsest," in *Naming the Rose: Essays on Eco's "The Name of the Rose,"* ed. M. Thomas Inge (Jackson: University Press of Mississippi, 1988), p. xv, n. 1.

16. *Deconstruction & Criticism*, ed. Geoffrey Hartman et al. (New York: Continuum, 1979), p. 150. He also cites Heidegger's text on "Die Rose ist ohne warum," from which the title for this chapter is taken.

Chapter XV

Roses and the Arts: A Humanistic and Horticultural *Engagement*

A unique but ultimately memorable conference was held at Central State University, in Wilberforce, Ohio, as well as in the nearby town of Xenia, on May 8, 1986. With its title as that given above, its educational town-and-gown purpose was multi-petaled: to honor rosarians, Central State's vigorous, young and new President (Arthur Thomas), Umberto Eco's *The Name of the Rose* (a bestseller now out in softcover), and to celebrate Emily Dickinson's hundredth anniversary the same month (her interest in roses being also well recognized). The theme was tempering Nature (as symbolized by the floral subject) through Art. Papers were delivered on famous American rose poets (Dickinson, Melville, Stein), rose art was on display, and slide presentations added another visual component. Among the leading exhibits was a painting entitled "Rose" (1850) by the nineteenth-century artist Robert S. Duncanson, the first Afro-American to attain fame as a landscape painter; it was acquired just prior to the conference from an anonymous Cincinnati donor. This extra was particularly relevant to the occasion insofar as Central State is a largely Afro-American university. And it was a good painting too.

Proceedings commenced on campus with a helpful overview of "The History and Romance of the Rose" by a locally renowned rosarian from the nearby locale of Bellbrook. Replete with slides, it showed how, as Miss Stein put it, civilization indeed began with a rose. The speaker told of how this flower had then been proposed as the national flower in Congress. Her own Fairy Rose had won "Best Show" in a recent exhibition in our area, which is extremely prominent nationally as a rose-growing one, the leading national prizewinner, Mrs. Betty Pavey, heralding from Xenia.

President Thomas's arrival resulted in several lively presentations, including one to him as "Mr. Rose." In recognition, he referred with gratitude to Jackson & Perkins, "World's Largest Rosegrowers and Nurserymen," who had donated one hundred and twenty rose bushes for this event. Two gardens had already been planted. Mrs. Pavey was likewise honored for being a distinguished rosarian, author of a book on rose display entitled *Say It with Roses*.

The second session, "Roses and American Literature," included James Hughes and William Baker of Wright State University, Dayton, specialists who spoke on Dickinson and Stein respectively, and Frank Henninger, Head of the American Studies Program at the University of Dayton, who related the rose metaphor more to a fictional person, Melville's "Jimmy Rose," in a paper called "The Budding of Melville's Third Phase." He showed how this short story astutely revealed the fiction writer's transitional style. Baker read his prose poem composed in the style of Stein, one composed on and published during the fiftieth anniversary of her death.

The third session, "Roses in Culture: Religion, Painting, Poetry, Music," commenced with the Rev. Théodore Koehler's after-luncheon address; Director Emeritus now of the largest Marian library, he dealt with "The Rose in Christian Western Iconography," showing how Christians throughout the ages have expressed their religious convictions with flowers. Qualifying his subject adroitly by observing that the rose was never as significant a symbol as the tree, lamb, or cross (except perhaps, ironically, for the Rosicrucians), he noted how it fails to appear as such in the Hebrew Bible or New Testament. Still, the Græco-Roman heritage stressing rose symbolism was then magnificently transformed by the Roman Church. Although Christ was sometimes symbolized as a rose, this Queen of Flowers was more often linked with Mary (both through the "rose garden" concept, as in Dante, and the rosary). Fr. Koehler considered the relevance of noted art works, such as the Schongauer Madonna (among the rocks) and the Dürer "Feast of the Rosary," wherein the Virgin hands out crowns of roses. This pictorial aspect was particularly fascinating in relation to the conference theme.

Chapter XV: Roses and the Arts

Following him, Bing Davis, Chair of the Art Department at Central State and a nationally known artist, related rose symbolism more to modern art, notably to the surrealistic painting of Salvador Dalí. This session included also oral interpretations of famous rose poems (including Frost's "The Rose Family") and songs (such as Louise Reichart's "In the Time of Roses"). Cecile Cary of nearby Wright State University, who had directed a sister conference a few years before, also funded by the OHC, called "Shakespeare and the Arts," served as an able moderator.

After a reception and inspection of one of the new rose gardens by a specialist from the University of Dayton, to provide more of the horticultural aspect, participants proceeded a few miles to Xenia for the final session at the Greene County District Library. The focus was more explicit than hitherto: Eco's *The Name of the Rose* (at the time being made into a costly film in Europe). Because of the novel's monastic setting and stress on a labyrinthine library with invaluable *manuscripta* (leading to a Gothic plot), the discovery of an *incunabulum* recently by the Chief Librarian at nearby Wilberforce University dovetailed beautifully. Being also on the Planning Committee, she displayed the *Scriptores reis Rustica* (Writings About Country Life), which perforce dealt in part with rose culture; printed in 1496 during the "cradle days of printing," this three-hundred-page volume was a notable find.

This last session dealt with contemporary interest in Eco's immense achievement (politically, semiotically, in terms of detective lore, and otherwise). Owing to his deliberate use of the Sherlock Holmes mythos, we focused on his novel as a Whodunit, Holmes and Watson being transformed into William of Baskerville and Adso(n). Serious papers were presented under the general rubric of "The 'Sherlockian' Background," but some question arose whether this work could be considered strictly a Holmesian pastiche because it does not adhere to the framework of the original model, except in a transmogrified manner.

The first speaker was the conference director and author of the present book; he focussed on this Stein-like theme: "A Rose Based on a Rose Based on a Rose: From Collins to Doyle to Eco"; the point was to show how Eco's rose derived from Doyle's "The Adventure of the Naval Treaty," which, in turn, owed much to Cuff's admiration of this flower in *The Moonstone* (see Chapter III). Because Holmes concentrated on the moss rose, the Name of the Rose was revealed as such. Passages in the novel "echoing" the sleuth's admiration for the rose include the following:

> (1) One day I observed [William] strolling in the flower garden without any apparent aim, as if he [like Holmes's rose] did not have to account to God for his works.
>
> (Prologue)[1]

> (2) "Frangula," William said suddenly, bending over to observe a plant that, on that winter day, he recognized from the bare bush. "A good infusion is made from the bark...."
>
> "You are cleverer than Severinus," I said to him, "but now tell me what you think of what we have heard!"
>
> (Second Day, Sext)[2]

It should hardly be necessary to gloss the similarities between these passages and the familiar rose digression in *The Naval Treaty* for most readers. The first passage suggests that the purpose of the rose is simply to reveal the love of God. Thus, Adso is somewhat critical of William when we compare him this way to Holmes with his rose. The second passage points to the *tone* of the passage in *The Naval Treaty*, whereby Holmes digressed from the main matter at hand, the treaty, to attend to his professed love of the flower; the ensuing impatience of the bystanders is likewise evidenced in Adso's exclamatory response in the rose novel. Because Eco has written on the Sherlock Holmes tradition elsewhere as well, these parallels were scarcely coincidental. He co-edited, for example, *The Sign of Three: Dupin, Holmes, Peirce.* Numerous other Sherlockian elements are present in the novel including (1) The "villain" Jorge, who is based primarily on Borges, but also recalls Von Herder, the blind German mechanic who craftily constructed Sebastian Moran's air-gun to the order of Professor Moriarty. Two reasons prompt this identification: Jorge is described as "that half-dead *German* with a *blind* man's eyes." (2) The sleuth, William, is akin to Sherlock, though the latter ironically retains more faith in Providence than does the former; whereas the former applies serendipity, Holmes operates on the grounds of "reasoned intuition" (which he calls deduction); Williams's physical features are akin to Holmes's: his slimness, hawk-like nose, and bony

Chapter XV: Roses and the Arts

hands; both are interested in scouting with lenses, the nature of poisons, prints in the earth, and the theft of important manuscripts; both are guilty of breaking and entering when necessary, and so forth. (3) William's partner or novice, Adso (originally called Adson, hence nominally like Watson), is somewhat akin to Sherlock's, especially in their being the lady's man upon occasion. (4) Perhaps the most unusually philosophic parallel is the following: the outset of the novel (the discovery of the MS containing the story then told by Adso) begins the customary way Sherlockian pastiches so often originate: by reference to a "new" tale located in Watson's so-called "lost box." Eco makes much of the *kind* of translation because doing so relates to his semiotic approach: he thus calls it a "translation of a translation" (thereby pointing to the perils in relating the thing named to the object itself); so his book, in dealing with a "lost" book, is said to become conscious of its own "bookness." But Adso's account is only an *attempt* to tell the truth and explain its mystery, even as language, Eco implies, is only an *attempt* to reflect the nature of reality.

The second speaker, Elizabeth Brinkman of Wittenberg University, commented expertly on "Adso: The Watson of the Piece?" She, too, felt that the key to the book is in the character of the narrator, the novice Adso, whose evolution is more profound than in that of Dr. Watson. On the other hand, the novel is still more Watsonian than Sherlockian, the focus being rather on the narrator (even if Watson is only a diminished counterpart of him) than the detective figure (who amounts more to an anti-detective type in the end). The third speaker, Pierre L. Horn of Wright State University (a native of Paris, France), related his title derived from Du Bellay to the Frenchified theme of the conference's subtitle: "... the Defense and Illustration of Humanism." His paper was then published in *Naming the Rose* as "The Detective Novel and the Defense of Humanism."[3] He went into depth in showing how William is superior to Jorge, largely because of his espousal of humanistic ideals. He recognized other influences (e.g. of Voltaire's *Zadig*) in passing. In discussion afterwards, it was noted that although, to be sure, William is better than Jorge, Adso is religiously superior to William (even if the Novice has always something to learn from his associate). For William has lost his faith in the end.

The fourth speaker, Alvin E. Rodin, M.D., one of the world's leading authorities on Conan Doyle, on whom he has written extensively, found many of the resemblances to the Sherlockian Canon superficial. His paper appeared afterwards, in revised form, in an issue devoted in part to the Eco novel in a leading, Chicago-based Doyle journal.[4] Guests at the session included Paul Herbert, a member of the famed Baker Street Irregulars from Cincinnati and authority on the writing of Sherlockian pastiches (being author of the leading and perhaps only book on the subject). This final session had been "previewed" at length earlier over station WYSO at Antioch College, with most participants present for a lively half hour's give-and-take, even as the entire conference was "previewed" for WCDR (Cedarville College) just before the first session (also with many morning participants present).

This conference is noteworthy to write up for other reasons as well. It included several participants from nearby Springfield, which was once known as "The Rose Capital of the World"; it was funded by the OHC in Columbus, only a bit further north, with its well-known Park of Roses. It was fitting that the event could be held when it was, as a prelude to the Mother's Day weekend, and that it could be partially funded by a grant from the Ohio Humanities Council, which applauded the results. All the papers from Session IV were requested for publication by *Baker Street Miscellanea* (Chicago), though finally only one (Dr. Rodin's) was printed there in revised form. The director's paper appeared in *The Sherlock Holmes Review* (Bloomington, Indiana).[5] The most notable publication was Pierre Horn's chapter in *Naming the Rose*.[6] As if to underscore the import of Eco's novel, but also this conference, that scholarly collection of essays was originally called *Anatomy of a Bestseller* and accepted by the Greenwood Press. Perhaps that title should have stuck, for, as it turned out, another book, also on Eco's novel, appeared at about the same time with the Cornell University Press; it, too, was called *Naming the Rose*. The result is almost a parody of semiotics itself. Fortunately it did not quite conflict with the title of the present volume.

Notes

1. *The Name of the Rose*, p. 10.
2. *The Name of the Rose*, p. 159.

Chapter XV: Roses and the Arts

3. *Naming the Rose,* pp. 90-100.
4. Alvin E. Rodin and Jack D. Key, "Some Comments on Sherlockian Similarities in Eco's *The Name of the Rose,*" *Baker Street Miscellanea* (Chicago), no. 47 (Autumn 1986), pp. 17–19.
5. As "The Master Sleuth Accommodated" cited earlier.
6. For a review of this book, one stressing Horn's chapter, see R. F. Fleissner's in *Baker Street Miscellanea,* no. 55 (Autumn 1988), pp. 47–48. The editor of the collection, M. Thomas Inge, has now informed me of still another such volume: *Ecos Rosenroman: Ein Kolloquium,* ed. Alfred Haverkamp and Alfred Heit (Munich: Deutscher Taschenbuch Verlag, 1987). For that matter, coincidentally enough a further book on Eco's novel, also called *Naming the Rose,* appeared at the same time as the Mississippi volume from the Cornell University Press—but avoids Holmes.

Program

Four sessions. Of these the first three are sponsored by the Department of English, Theatre, and Communication, Central State University, in conjunction with the Departments of Music, Art, and Biology and the Hallie Q. Brown Library; the fourth is sponsored by the Green County District Library, Xenia.

Exhibitions of works relating to roses and the arts, particularly painting and literature, will be on display in the Central State and Green County Libraries.

Registration. 9:30 to 10:50 am. The Wesley Room, CSU Library.

Session I. 10:00 to 10:50 am. (The Wesley Room, CSU library) Preliminary announcements. Robert F. Fleissner (Project Director, Central State University) Special presentations.

Roses for Art

Opening remarks. Terrence Glass (Chairperson, Department of English, Theatre, and Communication, Central State University)

Arthur E. Thomas (President, Central State University) Welcome

Mary Sherman (Bellbrook) The History and Romance of the Rose

(Moderator: Terrence Glass)

Session II. 11:00 to 12:15 pm. (The Wesley Room)

Roses and American Literature

James Hughes (Wright State University) "I bring my rose ...": Emily Dickinson's Gift of Power

Frank Henninger (University of Dayton) "Jimmy Rose": The Budding of Melville's Third Phase

W. Baker (Yellow Springs) Gertrude Stein's Roses

(Moderator: Alfreida Augman, Central State University)

Luncheon. Mercer Cafeteria, CSU (optional), 12:30 to 1:15 pm.
Book exhibit. Lobby, Robeson Center, 1:15 to 2:00 pm.

Session III. 2:00 to 3:30 pm, Paul Robeson Cultural and Performing Arts Center, Recital Hall (CSU)

Roses in Culture: Religion, Painting, Poetry, Music

Théodore Koehler (Director, Marian Library, University of Dayton) The Rose in Christian Western Iconography)

(Poetry reading, ETC Department, Central State University)

Willis (Bing) Davis (Central State University) Roses and Art

(Musical selections, Music Department, Central State University)

(Moderator: Cecile Cary, Wright State University)

Chapter XV: Roses and the Arts

Tea reception. Inspection of rose garden. The Music Library, Robeson Center, 3:45 to 4:15 pm.

Session IV.   4:45 to 6:00 pm. (Greene County Library Conference Room, Second Floor, Xenia)

> Preliminary announcements. Raymond Mulhern (Director, Greene County District Library, Xenia)
> *The 'Sherlockian' Background of Eco's* The Name of the Rose
> R. F. Fleissner (Project Director) A Rose Based on a Rose Based on a Rose: From Collins to Doyle to Eco
> Elizabeth Brinkman (Wittenberg University) Adso: The Watson of the Piece?
> Pierre L. Horn (Wright State University). *The Name of the Rose*: The Detective Novel and the Defense and Illustration of Humanism
>
> (Discussant: Alvin E. Rodin, M.D., Wright State University and Greene County Memorial Hospital)
>
> (Moderator: Ruth Colvin Central State University)

Reception hosted by the Greene County District Library. Book exhibit.

The Planning Committee

Chamness, Edward (Director, Informational Services, Central State U.)
Engel, Gertrude (Xenia)
Fleissner, R. F. (Project Director)
Glass, Terrence (Chairperson, ETC Dept., Central State University)
Johnson, G. T. (Director, Central State University Library)
Mulhern, Jean (Chief Librarian, Wilberforce University)
Mulhern, Raymond (Director, Greene County District Library)
Washington, William (Chairperson, Dept. of Biology, Central State University)
Yawn, Elizabeth (Major in English, Central State University)

Special thanks are due to Jackson & Perkins Co., World's Largest Rose Growers and Nurserymen.

Afterword

Robert Fleissner's floral and herbal survey of literature advisedly begins with Shakespeare and the rose because it is now published not many months after a very important archeological discovery in London: the finding of the remains of the sixteenth-century Rose Theatre on Bankside. There Shakespeare was in his early throes as actor and playwright on March 3, 1592, with one of his *Henry VI* plays, according to the account book of Philip Henslowe, who founded the theatre and opened it probably in 1587. It was named the Rose because it was built on a former rose garden; it is another historical circumstance that binds the great poet to the rose thematically. The foundations of the old theatre were located unexpectedly when an office building was torn down for a new construction. Immediately a campaign began to save these historical discoveries from disappearing anew under another building. A plan was soon underway to preserve them and to continue excavating all the ruins of the Rose. Devotees and members of professional learned societies, such as The Marlowe Society of America (of which Dr. Fleissner has been a member), have been encouraged to do all that they can to preserve these remains. Hence although his initial intent was not to relate his rose by another name to this theatre, his final intent—as specified in the Acknowledgments at the end of his Preface—is to have this book be supportive also of this fascinating archeological research.

Our own discovery of "a rose by another name" is encouraged with the help of a fine scholar as he decodes the message carried by flowers and herbs, particularly by the queen of flowers, the rose, in the work of poets and novelists and by means of scholarly and critical interpretation.

In this garden the reader is put in mind of a patient bee gathering nectar from rose to rose, from one flower to another to make its own delicious honey. A walk through Fleissner's garden may reconcile with modern hermeneutics those who shy away from such research. For when we read a text, when we look at a painting, are we not like Champollion, seeking to decipher an unknown language? But our language does not clone reality, the creation of God. We imitate, we copy, we alter, we transform this creation. But we have to thank the Creator who gave us such a reality; the rose needs a painter, a poet to give to God this answer. "Consider the lilies of the field.... I tell you, even Solomon in all his glory was not clothed as one of these" (Matt. 6. 28–29). Yes! In creation's beauty

"... a rose is a rose is a rose."

We hope that this study by Dr. Fleissner will help with the restoration of the 'Theatre of the Rose" in London; this venture on the rose symbol had a beginning in that long overlooked locale.*

June 1989　　　　　　　　　　　　The Rev. Théodore Koehler, S. M.

*The Rev. Koehler's paper, initially presented at the Rose Conference, has appeared as "The Christian Symbolism of the Rose" in *Our Lady's Digest*, 42 (1987), 17–25. (RFF)

The Black Rose

I seek the flower reflecting night
while others blaze with dyes of day.
That blackness lures me from the light.

Crowds of loud roses glut my sight.
From bed to bed eyes ricochet,
seeking the flower reflecting night.

Now, at a hundred Fahrenheit,
all petals sizzle in noon's ray
and blackness lures me from the light,

from roses yellow, red, and white
in sun that ovens brick from clay:
I seek the flower reflecting night.

I grow so dizzy with bloom too bright
(like a drunkard reeling from Tokay)
that blackness lures me. From the light,

color explodes—hushed dynamite
that blasts the mind. Turning away,
I seek the flower reflecting night.
That blackness lures me from the light.

     Alfred Dorn
     Director, World Order of
     Narrative Poets

Index

Key:

ACD = Arthur Conan Doyle
KK = "Kubla Khan"
S. H. = Sherlock Holmes
Shak = Shakespeare
STC = Samuel Taylor Coleridge
TSE = T. S. Eliot

Abrams, Meyer H., 66, name play on *petra* and *Peter*, 10; *KK*'s "Milk of Paradise," 63; opposed to late dating of *KK*, 71
Alexander, William, dependent on Shak, 125
Alford, Henry, on STC's veracity, 41
Amherst, Alicia, 18
Anatomy of a Bestseller, 142
Aquinas, Thomas, stress on sense data, 13; on stellar influence, 26
Arden (Shakespeare), Mary, 7–11, 15 n. 9
Aristotle, xv, 29, 80
Armour, Richard, 82, 84 n. 3; humorous variation on Stein, 80
Augman, Alfreida, 144

Aylmer, Felix, 57 n. 13

Baird, R. S. M., Mary Julian, 12, 15 n. 7; on the "joy of Rosalind," 14
Baker, William, Stein's roses, 138, 144
Banckes, Richard, 22–23
Baring-Gould, William, S.H. related to Sermon on the Mount, 46
Bate, A. Jonathan, 27; *Angelica* as herb or nurse, 29–30, 31 nn. 29–30
Bateson, F. W., 44 n. 15; source for STC's pronunciation of *Khan*, 65, 73 n. 6
Baudelaire, Charles, addicted to drugs, 63

151

Baum, L. Frank, TSE's debt to Oz, 100, 101 n. 6
Bazin, André, 40
Beer, J. B., opposed to late dating of *KK,* 71, 73 n. 6. *See also* Abrams, Meyer H.
The Bible, 48, 70, 133; *Wisdom of Solomon,* 3; *Song of Solomon,* 3, 132; *Matthew,* 10, 46; *Psalms,* 12; *Isaiah,* 105; Lord's Prayer, 126
Blake, William, xii, 35
Blakeney, T. S., on ACD and Collins, 50
Bleiler, Everett, vulgar overtones in Rosa Bud's nickname, 39
Bloom, James Harvey, 25, 30 n. 11; favoring monk's hood, 31 nn. 23–24
Boaz, Mildred Meyer, golden section proportionality in TSE, 98 n. 14. *See also* Fleissner, Robert F.
Bogdanovich, Peter, 57 n. 4
Booth, Stephen, Shak and doubling, 15 n. 2
Breitkreuz, Hartmut, "Rosebud" in STC, 44 n. 8
Bridgman, R., 88 n. 3
Brinkman, Elizabeth, 141; Eco's Adso as Watson type dominating, 145
Brinnin, Malcolm, toward Stein's third and fourth roses, 80, 84 n. 4
Brooker, Jewel Spears, on teaching Eliot, 98 n. 14

Brown, Ivor, on Maugham as unimpressed by Depth Psychology, 114
Burns, Robert, xii, 81, 87–88, 92–93
Burroughs, John, 60
Burt, Forrest D., 116 nn. 6, 11
Byron, Lord, debt to *KK,* 69–74

Campbell, M. L., Dickensian overtones in *Citizen Kane,* 57 n. 6
Canary, Robert H., "hollow" vs. "empty" meanings in "The Hollow Men," 99, 101 n. 2
Carringer, Robert L., Rosebud sled, 38; academic status given *Kane,* 43 n. 4; Hearst's own rosebuds, 55; "Rosebud" as Freudian, 56 n. 2. *See also* Freudianism
Carter, Annie Burnham, 30 n. 3
Cary, Cecile, xvi; director of "Shak and the Arts" conference, 139, 144
Chaucer, Geoffrey, on mint, 20; Marian imagery, 94; use of the pentad, 97 n. 10; his Miller akin to Emil Miller, 113
Chimes at Midnight, 54
Cirlot, J. E., symbolism of numbered rose petals, 77, 78 n. 2; Jungian symbolism in *Hollow* and

Index

Emptiness, 99–101. *See also* Jung, Carl
Citizen Kane, xiii, xv–xvii, xx, 38–40, 53–57. *See also* Welles, Orson; Mankiewicz, Herman
The Citizen Kane Book, 56 n. 1
Clairvaux, Bernard de, stress on *Solomon's Song* in homilies, 132. *See also* Morlay, Bernard de; The Bible
Coleridge, Samuel Taylor, xv, 38–39, 41–44, 55, 59–74; Shak as plant, 29; opium as the serpent in the garden, 59–67; Byron's debt to, 69–74
 "Kubla Khan," xv, xx, 41–44; Welles' debt to, 54–57
 "The Pains of Sleep," more dangers of opium, 66
 "The Rime of the Ancient Mariner," aesthetic moral, 65; Byron's debt to, 74 n. 12
Coles, W., 18
Collins, Wilkie, xi–xiii, 37, 45–51, 63
Colvin, Ruth, 145
Constable, Henry, xv–xvi, 119–29
Cook, Reginald L., published Frost's remarks on pentad, 96 nn. 2–3; chapter dedicated to him, 98
Crowley, Aleister, Maugham fascinated by his Satanism, his relation to Cronshaw, 110. *See also* Wilde, Soames, Morria
Cruz, Sor Juana Inés de la, xix
Cuff, Sergeant, 37; prototype of S. H. on roses, 45–52. *See also* Collins, Wilkie
Culpepper, 26

Dakin, D. Martin, xi; on the hypothesis of rose fragrance as attracting insect fertilizers, 47–48
Dante Alighieri, xii, 10–11, 135; Rose related to circle, 83, 95; TSE's rose related to Dante's Celestial, 101
Davis, Willis (Bing), rose symbolism in painting, 139, 144
De E Apud Delphum, classical pentad lore ("E" as fifth letter), 94
Dead? Or Alive?, variant title of *Edwin Drood*, 56
Deelman, Christian, 18
DeMaria, Jr., Robert, 32 n. 46
Demuth, Charles, "The Great Figure" (5), 92
DeQuincey, Thomas, opium-eater, 63
Deutsch, Babette, recognized Frost's roseate affinity with Dobson, 87
Devlin, Christopher, Hamlet's ghost's and Ophelia's rosemary-like allusions, 23, 31 n. 22

Dickens, Charles, xii–xiii, xv, 38–41, 51 nn. 10–11, 53–57
All the Year Round, 51 n. 10
"Another Whitstable Trade," 106
Bleak House, debt to Collins, 51 n. 10
David Copperfield, ACD's debt to, 51 n. 9; Maugham's use of, 104–7, 110–12, 114–16
Dombey and Son, Hearst's interest in, 55
Great Expectations, Philip akin to Pip, 106
"The Happy Fishing Grounds," 106
The Mystery of Edwin Drood, xii, xv, 38, 41, 51 n. 10; source for *Citizen Kane*, 54–57
Pickwick Papers, Welles's interest in filming, 54
Dickinson, Emily, 144; her centenary celebrated, 137
The Divine Comedy, xii, 10–12, 94, 101, 135. *See also* Dante Alighieri
Dobrinsky, J., Maugham in France, debt to Dickens, Mildred based on youth, 109, 116 n. 11
Dobson, Austin, Frost indebted to his rose imagery, xv, 87
Dodoens, Rembert, 27, 33
Donne, John, squaring Dante's circle again, 48; five as "true number" in "The Primrose," 93; basis for Frost's "Moon Compasses," 94, 97 n. 8; sexual overtones in death imagery, 126
Dorn, Alfred, xvi, 146
Doxey, William S., 96 n. 4
Doyle, Arthur Conan, xi–xiii, xvi, 37, 45–52; his names contrasted with Dickens's, 104; the S. H. tradition, 115 n. 3, 119; Eco's rose as derivative of ACD's, 139–42
"Gentlemanly Joe," 51 n. 10
The Man with the Twisted Lip, akin to Collins, 50
The Naval Treaty, rosarian digression akin to one in *The Moonstone*, 37, 45–52, 139
The Resident Patient, 50 n. 2
The Second Stain, the first stain being in Collins, 51 n. 12
The Sign of the Four, Collins-like Indian background, 49
"That Veteran," 51 n. 10
"Uncle Jeremy's Household," anticipatory of S. H., 49
Dreiser, Theodore, responsible for promoting *Bondage*, 113
The Dresser, unashamed use of British nickname, 40
Duffield, H., *Drood*'s debt to *Macbeth*, 55, 57 n. 8

Duncanson, Robert S., first African American landscape painter of repute, 137

Eagleson, Harvey, on Stein as unesoteric, 83, 84 n. 10
Eco, Umberto, 145; his bestseller, xiv–xv, xx, 25; more Watsonian than Sherlockian, 37; main focus at rose conference, 119; his "ambiguity" challenged, 131–36; debt to ACD, 139–42
Eliot, T. S., 75–77; rosarian debt to Dante, xii, xv; on *The Moonstone* as the greatest, Holmes akin to Cuff, 51 n. 11; on literature *qua* literature, 59; critical of *KK*, 64; akin to Stein, 83; satirized by Frost, 85; Frost and Burns related, 87; stress on Metaphysicals and Donne, 94; number mysticism, 98; hope in potentiality for fulfilment, 99–101
Four Quartets, xii, xiv, 83
"Hamlet and His Problems," 59
"The Hollow Men," 99–101
Introduction to Valéry's *Le Serpent*, 77
Selected Essays, 55 n. 11, 61 n. 1
The Waste Land, 99

"Wilkie Collins and Dickens," 51 n. 11
Ellacombe, Henry N., 30 n. 11
Ellmann, Richard, review of Eco's "delightful humor," 133
Encyclopedia of Gardening, the wild rose's customary five petals, 77
Evans, Maurice, use of 1592 *Diana* as base text, 122, 128 n. 2. *See also* Fleissner, Robert F.
Eyler, Ellen, 18, 32 nn. 42–43

Faulkner, William, a preserved rose for Emily, 132
Ferguson, Liane, *Angelica* as herb or nurse, 27, 31 n. 29
Ferruci, Franco, favorable review of Eco, 134
Fitz-Herbert, Sir Anthony, 33
Fleissner, Robert F. (monographs, articles, reviews, correspondence, etc.), letter on Shak's religion, 41; rev. on Oz and Alice, 41, 44 n. 16; "Uncle Jeremy's Household" as the original Baker Street mystery, 51 n. 8; directed *Angel Street*, 51 n. 11; query on "Rosebud" eliciting replies, 56 n. 1; Dickens's debt to Shak, 57 n. 7; onomastics in *Drood*, 57 n. 13; STC,

drugs, and the modern
world, 62 n. 2;
Tennyson's use of
Xanadu, 73 n. 2; Frost's
unconscious use of
number lore, 96 n. 1;
follow-up, 96 n. 3; Frost's
use of Donne, 97 n. 8;
Chaucer's and Goethe's
use of the pentad, 97 n.
10; TSE's use of Oz, 101
n. 6; Maugham's use of
Dickens, 116 n. 5; 1592
ed. of Constable's *Diana*
set up critically, 128 n. 1;
last line of *The Name of the
Rose*, 136 n. 5; Eco's debt
to ACD and Collins, 139,
143 n. 5, 145; rev. of
Naming the Rose, 143 n. 6
Fortin, René E., post-Edenic
imagery in Shak, 12
Fowler, Alastair, classic
pentad lore, 94, 97 n. 11
Fox, Helen Morgenthau, 32
n. 45
Fox, Levi, standard work on
Shak's flowers, 30 n. 11
Foxton, W., 30 n. 11
Freudianism, girl's suggestive
name in *Drood*, 39-40, 44
n. 11; "dollar book
Freud," 53, 56
Frick, Patricia Miller,
symbolism in *The
Moonstone*, 52 n. 12
Frost, Robert, xv, 77, 127,
139; variations in a rose
family, 85-98

"Acquainted with the
Night," debt to Dante,
94-95
"The Constant Symbol,"
reference to Dobson, 87
"The Gold Hesperidee,"
number lore, 91, 96 n. 1
"Moon Compasses," debt to
Donne, 94-95, 97
"Mowing," the fact as
sweetest, 95
"'Out, Out—,'" number
lore, 91
"The Road Not Taken,"
parodic occasion, 86
"The Rose Family," number
lore, xv, 85-98, 139
Frye, Northrop, debt of
Romantics to *KK*, 74 n. 12

Gambill, Norman Paul,
Welles's debt to Garland,
39, 44 n. 9
Garcia, S. Louise, drug
education, 44 n. 18
Gardener, Mayster J., his
limited availability, 31 n.
21
Garland, Hamlin, his Rose
book as influential on
Citizen Kane, 39
Gerard(e), John: standard
Renaissance work on
herbs, 21, 25, 27, 33
Gerber, Richard, the name
Kubla as akin to that of
Greek earth goddess, 71,
73 n. 10
Ghyka, Matila, the golden
section as operative in

Index

Nature, music, art, etc., 96, 97 n. 14
Gibson, John Michael, 51 n. 10
Glass, Terrence, 144–45
"Go, Lovely Rose," Waller's rose, xii
Goethe, Johann Wolfgang, Stein's debt to, 81; number lore, 97 n. 10; his debt to Spinoza, 105; on thorns with roses, 108; cited by Maugham, 114
The Golden Treasury, Frost's vade mecum, 87
"The Great Figure," 92, 96 n. 5
Greeley, Andrew, critical of Eco's semiotics, 131, 135
Green, Richard Lancelyn, 51 n. 10
Greene, Graham, ACD's mastery of roses, 103–4
Greenfield, Howard, Stein as serious on roses, 80–81, 84 n. 2
Grindon, Leopold Hartley, rosemary, 22, 30 n. 11
Grundy, Joan, imposition of the Dyce MS on Constable, 122–26
Gurr, Andrew, Hathaway and "hate away" related in Sonnet 145, 9

Haft, Adele J., vade mecum for reading Eco, 136 n. 11
Hall, Trevor H., TSE and ACD, 51 n. 11
Hamilton, Patrick, *Angel Street* as akin to Collins's work, 51 n. 11
Hammond, Gerald, Constable and Shak related, 124, 129 n. 9
Harbage, Alfred B., Shak and Dickens compared, 57 n. 7. *See also* Fleissner, Robert F.
Hardy, Thomas, *Tess* as influential on Maugham, 114
Hartman, Geoffrey, 136 n. 16
Hathaway, Anne, name play on her in Sonnet 145, 9
Haverkamp, Alfred, German papers on Eco, 143 n. 6
Hayter, Alethea, leading literary drugtakers, 63–64, 66 n. 1
Hearst, William Randolph, source for *Citizen Kane*, 41, 55–57
Heidegger, Martin, *Die Rose ist ohne warum* (the rose has no why or wherefore), 136 n. 16
"Heidenröslein," Goethe's rose, 81, 108
Heit, Alfred, German study of Eco, 143 n. 6
Hemingway, Ernest, "modernist" (or primitive), 81
Hennelly, Jr., Mark M., mysticism in *The Moonstone*, 51 n. 12

Henninger, Frank, rose metaphor in Melville, 138, 144
Herbarium, Old English herbal, 27
Herbert, George, "The Rose," 1
Herbert, Paul, B. S. I, 142
Herbert, Rosemary, Brett on Holmes in a rose garden, 50
Herrick, Robert, xix, 39
Higham, Charles, 43 n. 5, 57 n. 6
Hill (Hylle), Thomas, 33. *See also* Mountain, Didymus
Holmer, Joan Ozark, 32 n. 38
Holmesworth, Leonard, holy thistle, 20–21, 30 n. 11, 31 nn. 15–16
Honigmann, E.A.J., Shak's early Catholicism, xiv, xvii n. 7
Horn, Pierre L., xvi; Foreword, xix–xx; Shak and the *Song of Roland*, 15 n. 6; Ronsard, 43 n. 7; Eco and humanism, 141, 145
Hotta, Kimiko, 32 n. 36
Hsüan-chi, Yü, xx
Hughes, James, Dickinson's centenary, 138, 144
Hughey, Ruth, critical of the Dyce MS of the *Diana*, 122–23, 129 n. 7
Hyams, Edward, 18

Inge, M. Thomas, editor of critical study of Eco, 136 n. 15, 143 n. 6

"Jimmy Rose," Melville's rose variation, 138, 144
Johnson, Pamela Hansford, David as "Daisy," 116 n. 10
Johnson, Thomas, 33
Jones, William M., Shakespeare as the character William, 14 n. 2
Jordan, Frank, 22
Joyce, James, 9; use of *Hamlet* in *Ulysses*, 111. *See also Ulysses*
Jung, Carl, anima, 72; TSE's possible knowledge of, 77, 99. *See also* Cirlot, J. E.

Kant, Immanuel, bearing on Eco, 132
Kaufmann, Stanley, opposed to "Rosebud" as Freudian, 40, 44 nn. 13–14
Keats, John, 79; drugtaker, 63; dark Romantic beauty, 71
Keller, Gottfried, hay, herbs, and roses, 26
Kenilworth, The Gardens of, possibly known to Shak, 18
Key, Jack D., 143 n. 4
Kilmer, Joyce, arboreal vegetation, 86
Kincaid, Arthur, director of English acting group, 13
Knight, G. Wilson, 57 n. 8
Koehler, S.M., Théodore, 135, 138, 144; Christian iconography and the rose, 147–48

Index

Kurtz, Elizabeth Carney, 135 n. 4. *See also* Faulkner

Lacnunga, eleventh-century herbal, 24
Land, Herman W., 44 n. 18
Langham, William, 33
Leaming, Barbara, Welles, not Mankiewicz, as an originator of *Kane* idea, xiii, xvii n. 6; 43 n. 5
Lee, Sidney, Shak's MSS and pirating, 123
Lemnius, L., 23, 33
Levin, Harry, Shak's onomastics, 14 n. 1
Levith, Murray J., Shak's onomastics again, 14 n. 1
Liljegren, S. B., ACD's debt to Collins, xii, xvi n. 4, 50
Linden, Stanton J., 32 n. 32
Lowes, John Livingston, seminal source-hunting, 42, 63
Lyons, Clifford, friend of Frost, 88 n. 6
Lyte, Henry, 27, 33

McCombie, Frank, 32 n. 34
Macer, Aemilius, 23
McFarland, Thomas, 42, 74 n. 12
MacLeish, Archibald, 79–80, 85
Maison Rustique, 18
Malherbe, François de, xix
Mankiewicz, Herman, xiii, 38, 40; as general originator of "Rosebud," 53–56

Margoliouth, H. M., drinking-can named after *Khan*, 71, 73 n. 7
Mariology, 138, 147–48; Marian allusions in *As You Like It*, 3–11; Marian allusion in *Sir Gawayne*, 94. *See also* Chaucer, Geoffrey
Maugham, W. Somerset, xv, 78
  Beauty for Ashes, debt to Bible, Spinoza, 105
  Books and You, Dickens as "England's greatest novelist," 104
  Cakes and Ale, 114, Rosie, 108
  The Magician, based on Crowley, 110
  Of Human Bondage, xv, xx; Rose as male name, etc., 103–16
  The Summing Up, use of Spinoza, Trollope as more realistic than Dickens, 104–6
Maxwell, James F., meaning of "Rosebud," 53, 57 n. 3
Melville, Herman, 137–38, 144
Miller, Bruce E., 73 n. 5
Milner, Richard, S. H. and the rose, 52 n. 13
Milton, John, 11, 127; source for *KK*, 70. *See also Paradise Lost*
Montrose, Adrian, Shak's garden, 28, 32 n. 35

The Moonstone, xi, 45–52, 139. *See also* Collins, Wilkie
Moore, Thomas, dark Romantic beauty, 71
Morgan, Ted, provocative views of Maugham, 109; Maugham as related to Dickens, 116 n. 6
Morlay, Bernard de, rose reference at the end of Eco's novel, 131–32. *See also* Clairvaux, Bernard de
Morria, James, decadent prototype of Cronshaw, 110. *See also* Wilde, Oscar; Soames, Enoch; Crowley, Aleister
Morrissey, Charles T., on end-stops in Frost, 97 n. 8
Moses, Grandma, 81
Mountain, Didymus, 30 n. 2, 33. *See also* Hill, Thomas
Mulhern, Raymond, 145
Myer, Michael Grosvenor, origin of "Daemon Lover," 73 n. 11
"My Lady's Presence Makes the Roses Red," Constable's rose, xv, 119–29
Mysticism, xiv–xv, 3–15, 46–49, 83–84, 94; basis for Holmes's rose-mysticism, 51 n. 12; Dante's Mystical Rose, 65, 83, 94; hollowness as mystical, 99–101, 120. *See also* Dante Alighieri, *The Divine Comedy,* Neo-Pythagoreanism

Naked Lunch, 60
The Name of the Rose, xiv–xv, xx, 37; the name of the moss-rose, 50, 139, 143 n. 4, 145. *See also* Eco
Naming the Rose, 134, 136 n. 15, 142
Neo-Pythagoreanism, xv; subliminal usage in Frost, 91–98; William Carlos Williams's pentad, 92, 97 n. 5; Plutarch's pentad, 94; Renaissance number lore, 127. *See also* Mysticism
Newdick, Robert S., Frost's early biographer on Dobson, 88, 89 n. 9
Newman, Lucile F., 32 n. 39
Newton, biblical herbal, 22
Nichols, Beverley, Maugham's bondage, 109, 116 n. 12
Norden, Linda Van, 132, 136 n. 6
North, Michael, on Williams's pentad, 97 n. 5. *See also* Williams, William Carlos

Ober, William B., Keats and the "rose of love," 64, 67 n. 2
Older, Fremont, Hearst's biographer, 55, 57 nn. 9, 11–12
"O My Luv's like a red, red rose," Burns's rose, xii, 81

Index

Onomastics, xv; autobiographical and religious overtones, 3–15; clues for identifying the name *Rosebud*, 53–57; Stein's woman called Rose, 81–82, 86; Dobson's woman called Rose, 87; Frost's rose name, 95; a bondage to onomastics in Maugham, 103–16; Rose and Rosie, 108–109; Eco's naming, 119, 131–36 *et passim*. *See also The Name of the Rose*

d'Orléans, Charles, xx

Orwell, George, on Dickens as akin to Dalí, 104

Otten, Charlotte F., 27, 31 nn. 27–28

Ovid, 21

The Oxford Book of English Verse, 87

Pacioli, Fra Luca, 97 n. 14

Paget, Sidney, illustration of Holmes sniffing rose, 50

Paradise Lost, 11, 70. *See also* Milton, John

Parkinson, John, 27, 29, 33

Patterson, Jr., Charles I., STC's *demon* or *Daemon*, 60, 62 n. 3

Paul, St., seeing through "a glass darkly," 48. *See also* the Bible

Pavey, Betty, authority on rose arrangement, xiv, 138

Perrine, Laurence, Frost's roses, 97 n. 6

Peters, Ellis, 131

Plat, Sir Hugh, 29

Pliny, 20

Plutarch, 94

Poe, Edgar Allan, ACD's debt to, xi, 51 n. 12; intoxication, 63, 66; Stein-like repetition of word, 82; Marie Rogêt, 111

Poole, Eric, on the earliest document relating to ancestors of Shak, 15 n. 9

Postscript, 37, 131, 134. *See also* Eco, *The Name of the Rose*

Quigley, Michael, drug education, 44 n. 18

Redmond, Donald A., 115 n. 3

Reichart, Louise, 139

Reichert, Victor, "Directive" as related to TSE, 97 n. 9

Rennick, Robert M., meaning of Rosa Bud's nickname, 40, 44 n. 11

Rilke, Rainer Maria, 39, 117

Robertson, Jean, on Dorothy Wordsworth's "*Kubla*," 71, 73 n. 9

Rodin, Alvin E., 141–42, 143 n. 4; Eco's novel contrasted with a true pastiche, 145

Rogers, Robert, Shak's metaphoric rose culture, 32 n. 37

Rohde, Elinour Sinclair, 20, 31 nn. 13, 19–20, 25, 32

n. 44 *et passim;* Shak's monopoly on herbal references, 17
Le Roman de la Rose, 134
Ronsard, Pierre, 39, 43 n. 7
"The Rose," George Herbert's rose, 1
"A Rose for Emily," Faulkner's rose, 132
Rose of Dutcher's Coolly, Garland's rose book, 39
Rose Theatre, The, xvi, 133, 147–48
Ross, Jr., Donald, Wordsworth's debt to *KK,* 69, 73 n. 1
Ryan, Lawrence V., rehabilitating Eliot's Hollow Men, 99, 101 n. 1
Rydén, Mats, major work on Shak's plants, 18

Savage, Frederick G., 18, 31 nn. 17, 26
Sayers, Dorothy, S. H. and rose culture, 37; S. H. and Sgt. Cuff, 46
Say It with Roses, xiv, 138
Schneider, Elizabeth, 71, 73 n. 6; STC as prevaricator, 63–64
Schulz, M., 42
Scofield, Martin, critical of Joyce on *Hamlet,* 13
Scott, Walter, "The Daemon Lover," 73 n. 11
Scott, William O., flowers in *The Winter's Tale,* 30 n. 2
Scoufos, Alice-Lyle, terrestrial paradise in Shak, 15 n. 6

Seward, Barbara, previous book-length study of rose symbolism, 17
Seymour-Smith, Martin, argues for Maugham's ambisexuality, 114
Shakespeare, William, xiv, xvi, 50 n. 7, 54, 57 n. 7, 119, 147; woman as rose, xii; anagogical rose symbolism, 1–15; herbal culture, 17–33; sonnets related to Constable's, 123–27
All's Well That Ends Well, 20
As You Like It, xii–xiii, 3, 7–15, 19
The Comedy of Errors, 19
Hamlet, 13, 23, 28, 31 n. 27, 32 nn. 34, 36, 39; 59
1 Henry IV, 20
2 Henry IV, 25
Henry V, 20
3 Henry VI, 19
Julius Caesar, 100
King Lear, 20, 25, 32 n. 34
A Lover's Complaint, 21
Love's Labour's Lost, 20, 28
Macbeth, 19, 25, 54–55
The Merchant of Venice, 19
Measure for Measure, xiv, xix
The Merry Wives of Windsor, 19, 54
A Midsummer Night's Dream, 24, 32 n. 41
Othello, 19, 28, 32 n. 38, 126
Richard II, xii
Romeo and Juliet, xii–xiii, xv, xx, 4–5, 17–33, 124, 132–33

Index

The Sonnets, 1, 9, 122–27
Troilus and Cressida, 19
Twelfth Night, 4
The Two Gentlemen of Verona, xx
The Winter's Tale, 4, 20, 27, 30 n. 2, 32 n. 32
Shakespeare: The Lost Years, xiv
Shaw, John Bennett, ACD's names vs. Dickens's, 103–4, 115 n. 2
Shelley, Mary, dark Romantic beauty, 71
Shelley, Percy B., 74 n. 12
Sherman, Mary, overview of rose culture, 137, 144
"The Sick Rose," Blake's rose, xii
The Sign of Three, 140
Sir Gawayne and the Grene Knight, Marian imagery, 94
Sitwell, Edith, *The Canticle of the Rose*, 75
Slater, Michael, critical of Agnes, 115, 116 n. 19
Smith, C. Roach, 28, 32 n. 33
Soames, Enoch, 110. *See also* Wilde, Oscar; Crowley, Aleister; Morria, James
Solt, Mary Ellen, xx
The Song of Bernadette, xi
Soulé, Katherine, Hearst's childhood friend, 55
Spenser, Edmund, 127
Spiegelman, Willard, rose imagery in Keats and Shak, 50–51

Spinoza, Baruch, his *Ethics* influential on Goethe, 105
Spurgeon, Carolyn, Shak's imagery, 28
Stein, Gertrude, xiv–xv, 75, 77, 88; her four roses decoded, 79–86; debt of Frost to her, 92–93; cited by Eco, 134; more roses based on Stein's, 137–39
Strong, Roy, structure in Renaissance gardens, 27, 32 n. 31
Strothmann, Friedrich W., rehabilitating Eliot's Hollow Men, 99, 101 n. 1
Suther, Marshall, STC indebted to himself, 64, 71
The Symbolic Rose, 17
Symons, Julian, S. H. and Sgt. Cuff, 47, 50 n. 5

Tani, Stefano, Eco's novel and the anti-detective genre, 52 n. 13
T'ao, Hsüeh, xix
Taylor, Norman, wild roses as five-petaled, 77
Tennyson, Alfred Lord, debt to KK, 69, 73 n. 2
Thomas, Arthur E., 137–38, 144
Thomas, Edward, 86
Thompson, James, drugtaker, 63
Thompson, Lawrance, Frost vs. TSE, 87, 88 n. 5
Three Lives, 83, 86

"To the Virgins to Make
    Much of Time," Herrick
    on gathering rosebuds,
    39
Toole, William B., growth
    through adversity in
    Shak, 28, 32 n. 40
Tracy, Jack, 43
Treveris, Peter, 33
Trollope, Anthony, as more
    realistic than Dickens,
    104
Truffaut, François, 40
Turner, William, father of
    English botany, 22–23, 31
    n. 18, 33
Tusser, Thomas, 33

Ulysses, 9, 17, 111

Valéry, Paul, TSE's use of, 77
Viereck, Peter, parody of
    Kilmer, 86
A *Village Romeo and Juliet*, 26
Vittoz, Roger, TSE's Swiss
    doctor, 77
Vlasopolos, Anca, 28, 32 n. 41
Voltaire, François, *Zadig*, 141
Vyvyan, John, 32 n. 37

Wallace, David A., on Holmes
    as rose-lover, 50
Waller, Edmund, xii
The Way of All Flesh, 107
Weales, Gerald, on Welles, 43
    nn. 5–6
Webster, Helen Noyes, 30 n. 2
Welles, Orson, xiii, 38–41, 43–
    44, 53–57; debts to STC
    and Dickens, xv–xvii. *See*
    also Citizen Kane,
    Mankiewicz, Herman
Wentersdorf, Karl P., 27, 31 n.
    27
Werfel, Franz, xi
Wilde, Oscar, 109–10. *See also*
    Soames, Enoch; Crowley,
    Aleister; Morria, James
Wilder, Thornton, Stein's
    own evaluation of her
    roses, 86
Williams, William Carlos, 80,
    92, 96 n. 5
Winn, Dilys, detectives and
    flora, 52, n. 13
Wolfe, Nero, zest for orchids,
    37
Wordsworth, Dorothy,
    "*Kubla*" to a fountain, 71–
    72
Wordsworth, William, 35
    (headnote), 41, 65, 72,
    92; debt to *KK*, 69
Wyer, Robert, 23

Yachnin, Paul, *Angelica* as
    herb or nurse, 27, 31 n.
    29
Yarlott, Geoffrey, *KK* and
    STC's life, 64–66, 67 nn.
    3–5

Zadig, 141